Dance of the Third-string Quarterback

Dance of the Third-string Quarterback

A novel

Rod Vick

Laikituk Creek Publishing

Dance of the Third-string Quarterback
A novel

Laikituk Creek Publishing
Mukwonago, Wisconsin

This is a work of fiction. Names, characters, places, and incidents either are the product of the author's imagination or are used fictitiously. Any resemblance to actual persons, living or dead, events, or locales is entirely coincidental.

All rights reserved.
Copyright © 2008 by Rod Vick

Cover design Copyright © 2008 by Rod Vick

No part of this book may be reproduced or transmitted in any form or by any means, electronic or mechanical, including photocopying, recording, or by any information storage and retrieval system, without the written permission of the author, except where permitted by law.

Manufactured in the United States of America

ISBN: 978-0-6923173-9-6

For Josh, my son.

Note from the author

Irish dance has become a full-blown phenomenon. *Riverdance* helped make it so by boosting interest in Celtic culture, but the beauty, athleticism and passion inherent in competitive Irish dance have helped it to become self sustaining. Each year in north America, about two hundred feiseanna—or Irish dance competitions—take place, featuring the talents of anywhere from several hundred to more than two thousand dancers.

While girls still make up the largest contingent of Irish dancers, the number of boys continues to grow. My son started to dance at age twelve, and today, at age fourteen, he insists that Irish dance has dramatically improved his foot speed as a soccer player.

Still, boys and dance are often only dimly understood by outsiders, and many unfavorable stereotypes exist. This is not an anti-football book. Stereotyping can exist whenever different worlds collide. And this is a book about colliding worlds—Irish dance and football. While each exhibits its own unique athleticism, both sports are alike, too. Both Irish dance and football require diligent practice and hard work. Both are steeped in tradition.

And their participants are passionate and proud.

Rod Vick

Things do not change.
We change.

– Henry David Thoreau

One

Pilots! Pilots! Pilots!

Four hundred young men marched into the Paavo High School gymnasium. Most wore t-shirts and jeans. Some had smooth, pimply faces that would have seemed more at home hovering above a sandbox. Others wore the rough stubble of early maturity, and a few even showed the thin beards and hard features of adults. All chanted the school's team name as they marched.

Pilots! Pilots! Pilots!

The larger boy at Seth's right nudged his shoulder. "Isn't this awesome?" Seth had met Brandon Hardy at school registration three days earlier, and since he was one of the few familiar faces in the four hundred, Seth was drawn to him in the line of boys now heading into the gym. "It's like marching into the stadium at the Olympics!"

Seth eyed his new friend warily. "They don't have football in the Olympics. At least not the American type of football."

Brandon inched ahead, twisting his head in Seth's direction. "What type do they have?"

"They have soccer," said Seth. "Outside of the U.S., soccer is called football. So they have football in the Olympics. Just not the kind we play."

Brandon rolled his eyes. "Forget it! I feel like I'm marching into . . . the Super Bowl! They have football there, right?"

Seth laughed. "Between the TV commercials."

Brandon let the rush of crowd noise roll over him.

"This sure is different than the first day of football at St. Augustine," said Seth, his eyes still scanning the crowd.

Brandon scrunched his face. "What's St. Augustine?"

Seth was certain he had told Brandon before, but the little community four hours north of Paavo was not the sort of place people easily remembered. "It's where I went to school before we moved here. We only had about forty football players in grades nine through twelve."

His stocky, dark-haired friend rolled his eyes. "A hundred freshmen come out for the team here each year! How big is St. Asthma?"

"St. Augustine. I guess there were about a hundred and ninety in the high school."

Brandon emitted a tiny, surprised laugh. "I think Paavo's debate team is bigger than that! But then again, we're only a half hour from Milwaukee. Everything's bigger in this part of the state."

Seth recalled that on the first day of practice at St. Augustine, they had run for twenty minutes in t-shirts and shorts and then the three coaches had put them through a series of agility drills to test their quickness and coordination.

Paavo High School had nearly two thousand students and there had to be at least a dozen football coaches. So far, the first day of football seemed more like a rock concert than a practice.

The two boys found seats on the fifth row of the wooden bleachers in the "varsity" section, which was where juniors and seniors had been directed by the coaches. On the other side of the gymnasium sat the freshmen and sophomores. The wooden basketball court in between held green metal folding chairs for the coaches as well as another row for a group of young men about Seth's age.

"Those are the studs from last year's team," Brandon said, pointing and almost screaming to be heard above the din. "Some were all-conference! I think one was honorable mention all-state!" Seth counted nine studs.

When the last of the students had been seated, each coach stood in front of a chair and a whistle sounded. As if a switch had been flipped, all the chatter stopped instantly. At the same time, the lights went out, and the gymnasium was plunged into darkness.

A voice boomed over the public address system. "Gentlemen! Welcome to Pilot football!"

It IS like a rock concert, thought Seth.

Now a bright image lit up a movie screen that had been set up at one end of the gymnasium. Bodies crashed against one another, footballs sliced the air, running backs raced down the field to plunge into the end zone. The loudest music Seth had ever heard blared in the background.

After fifteen minutes of these highlights, the screen went dark and as the gym lights blinked on, the players applauded, cheered and pumped their fists. But they quieted again as Coach Blair approached a standing microphone set in front of the chairs.

"Welcome again, gentlemen!" He began in a friendly, confident tone, and Seth could see immediately how players liked this man and would follow him up a mountain. "I hope you enjoyed those clips from last season. We were a pretty good team. Finished second in the conference. Made it to the second round of the state playoffs. Finished with a 9-3 overall record."

Brief applause, mostly from the underclassmen, interrupted these remarks.

"Most of you know," he continued, "that we have a pretty high standard here at Paavo. Second isn't good enough. And our goal every year is to reach the state finals in Madison. I think this is going to be a very special year for Pilot football. At this time, I'd like to introduce some of the people who I believe will help make this happen."

Coach Blair introduced each of the players in the green chairs, having the athlete stand and then reciting his accomplishments. *No wonder Coach is pumped about this year,* thought Seth.

Introduced last was Jason Troy. "Last year as a sophomore," said Coach Blair proudly, "Jason became our starting quarterback, threw six touchdown passes and earned honorable mention to the all-conference team. He's a heck of an athlete and a competitor, and we expect big things from him this season."

The team gave Jason a hero's ovation.

Coach Blair then introduced the rest of the coaching staff—which took awhile—and finished with an inspirational story about a kid, years ago, who had been completely physically inept as a freshman. He offered numerous examples of his incompetence and failures, which earned laughter from the four hundred in the bleachers. "But he had heart and determination," noted the coach, "and he never gave up." Ultimately, the unnamed loser had morphed into a superb football-playing machine and had earned a scholarship to play ball at a small college. "That should be your goal," concluded Coach Blair. "To be better when you leave this team than you were the day you walked into this gymnasium. It's all up to you and how hard you're willing to work!"

Assistant Coach Wisk then rose from his seat. "Freshmen and sophs, get your shorts and jogging shoes on and report to the track! Upperclass, report to the equipment room!" He blew his whistle and the gym burst into movement.

"We're going to win state!" said Brandon as they lurched down the bleachers and headed toward the equipment room. "With all those good guys coming back and a great quarterback—and you and me—we can't lose!"

Seth smiled wanly, feeling like a leaf being swept along in a cyclone.

"I'm gonna be a lineman," continued Brandon as they passed through the double doors that led to the hallway where a line was now forming. "You probably guessed that by my size."

Seth smiled. "I kind of figured."

"How about you?" asked Brandon. "At that old school of yours, what position did you play?"

Seth smiled again, though sheepishly this time. "Quarterback."

Brandon's own smile disappeared. "That's too bad."

Now Seth shrugged. "I'm not worried. Every team needs a good backup quarterback. It'll give me a chance to learn Paavo's system."

Brandon nodded but not enthusiastically. "That's true. But Paavo's got a backup already. Danny Sidowski."

Seth sighed. "Is he any good?"

"Yeah," said Brandon. "Pretty good. But he's also something else that'll make it almost impossible for you to beat him out."

Seth steadied himself as the line surged forward. "What do you mean?"

"He's Jason Troy's best friend."

Two

"All right, let's see what you mushrooms can do!" shouted Coach Wisk.

Seth gave Brandon a sideways look.

"That's what Coach Wisk calls everyone until they do something good," Brandon explained. "I guess 'cuz mushrooms just sort of sit there and do nothing."

After the previous day's film and introductions, the freshman, junior varsity and varsity teams had all practiced together in helmets, shorts and t-shirts. Today everyone was in full equipment, and the juniors and seniors had been separated from the less experienced players. Seth looked forward to showing that he could fit in with the Pilots. He was more nervous than he had ever been at St. Augustine.

"Ready!" Coach's voice barked the command, and a line of about ten players settled into their three-point stance on the goal line. The whistle sounded and the ten exploded up the field, sprinting across the forty-yard line.

"Nice job Harding!" called Coach Wisk, acknowledging the winner of the sprint. "Schoelburg, group two."

Number eighty-seven hung his head, and Seth guessed this must have been Schoelburg, who had finished last in the sprint. That meant he would move "down" to group two.

A second group launched. "All right, Matters! You're up to group one! Horne, you're group three!"

There were eight groups. The first three seemed to be composed of players who had been around for awhile or whose reputations made them instantly recognizable. For the more obscure players in the later groups, Coach Wisk began to use the numbers on their practice jerseys. Seth was in group six.

"Six, on the line!"

Seth crouched, and at the whistle, he tore down the field.

"Number twenty-three, you're up a group! Sixty-seven, down!"

Seth's number was eight. As far as he could tell, he had finished second.

Maybe next time.

After the eighth group went, Coach Wisk called the first group to the forty-yard line and had them race back to the goal line. When all eight groups had done this, he raced them back to the forty again. They repeated this drill six times, and Seth was happy to have moved up to group four.

Brandon remained in group six.

Those guys in group one must have rockets!

Next, the team was divided into linemen and backs. The linemen—frequently the heavier, more thickly-muscled kids—went to the far end of the practice field with coaches Bartholomew and Kramer. The smaller, leaner backs stayed with Coach Wisk, Coach Westby and Coach Blair.

"All right mushrooms, we're going to see if any of you can catch!" brayed Wisk.

The backs formed two lines, one on the right and one on the left. Coach Westby, who looked to be about twenty-five and was the youngest on the Paavo staff, stood in the middle on the goal line. At the whistle, a player from each side would sprint fifteen yards down the field and then cut toward the middle for about five yards. Coach Westby would throw to one of them. Each catch was greeted with cheers. Each drop elicited the requisite groans and a round of criticism from Coach Wisk.

Seth caught his first ball, jogged to the end of the line on the other side, and then caught that one, too, when his turn came again.

Coach Wisk looked at his clipboard. "Not bad . . . number eight!"

This isn't so hard, he thought. *Not much different from St. Augustine.*

Then Coach Blair had them do the same drill, but two boys played defense against each back running a pass pattern. When it came time for Seth to run his route, he recognized Danny Sidowski lined up to defend.

It'd be sweet if I could catch one against him. Maybe Coach Wisk would start remembering my name!

At the signal, he sprinted downfield fifteen yards and cut toward the middle. The ball hung in the air right in front of him.

Easy catch!

Seth reached for the ball, but just as it touched his outstretched fingers, a freight train hit him from behind, driving him hard into the practice turf. The ball wobbled harmlessly away.

"Attaboy, Danny!" called Coach Wisk. "Nice crunch! You other boys take notice."

Seth picked himself up, prepared to take his position as a defender on the next play. As Danny Sidowski jogged past him toward the back of the line, he called out, "Welcome to Pilot football!"

A few of the others laughed.

Shake it off, Seth told himself. Moments later, a kid from the seventh sprint group caught a pass in front of him.

The practice ended at ten-thirty. They had started at eight. There were blocking drills, agility tests, tackling and lots of running.

"See you back here at five this evening," Coach Wisk reminded them as they left the field. "Remember, we train twice a day until school starts in September!"

Three weeks! Seth thought. *I hope I can survive that long!*

In the locker room, Brandon requested that no heroic measures be used to save his life. He lay on the bench like a displaced manatee. "Pull the plug! Let me die! Modern medical science can only prolong my agony!"

He felt a little better after a half-hour shower, but both boys were slow walking to the parking lot. Seth accepted the offer of a ride home from Brandon, but instead of a straight shot, Brandon pulled into The Hangar, a fast food and ice cream restaurant just a block away from the high school.

"I need something cold," said Brandon. "I'm buying."

Seth ordered a chocolate malt.

"So," began Brandon when they were seated at a table with their drinks, "how do Paavo's practices compare to St. Awkward's?" He pointed to the large, black letter A on his friend's school jacket.

"St. Augustine," Seth corrected him. Then he paused thoughtfully before answering. "In a lot of ways, it was the same. But there's more big guys here in Paavo. And more really fast guys. And—"

Brandon paused over his drink. "And what?"

"Well, so far it doesn't feel as friendly. But that's to be expected, right? I hardly know anybody."

"I heard you got to know Danny Sidowski," said Brandon. "He was telling some guys in the locker room how he splattered the new kid all over the field."

Seth felt the ache in his ribs and realized this was probably not much of an exaggeration.

"I'm still walking."

Brandon nodded, and then another question seemed to come to him. "So how come you guys moved? What's Paavo got that St. Augustine doesn't? Besides malls, movie theaters, street lights and indoor plumbing?"

Seth smiled. "We had those things up north. You just had to drive a little farther to get to them." Then he thought for a moment and added, "Not the indoor plumbing." Both boys laughed and Seth continued. "My dad died last year."

Brandon suddenly looked stricken. "Geez, I'm sorry. I didn't mean to . . ." His voice trailed off.

"It's pretty hard sometimes," Seth admitted in a low voice. "Especially since he was my coach."

Brandon seemed surprised. "Football?"

Seth nodded. "He was an assistant for the Ospreys—that's the St. Augustine team mascot. When he died, my mom moved us to Paavo. She grew up not far from here, so we've got plenty of relatives in this part of the state. I guess she felt all alone in St. Augustine without dad."

Brandon stirred his drink with a straw. "Do you wish you were still there?"

Seth sighed. "I wish my dad were still around."

"I mean, do you miss it? Your old team?"

Seth took a sip of his malt. "I haven't had enough time to *really* miss it. But I still *kind of* miss it. You know what I mean?"

Brandon shook his head yes but then said, "No. I think Danny Sidowski must have hit you way too hard!"

Seth smiled. "It was a hard hit. And like I said, there's a lot of big, fast players on the Pilots."

"Don't worry," said Brandon. "Even if we just sit the bench all year, the girls go crazy over football players at this school. We're going to have a great time!"

"But I don't want to sit the bench," said Seth.

"Well, then you better have some sort of secret weapon, because making the starting lineup on the Paavo football team is like running barefoot through fire!"

Seth noisily drained his malt cup, and then an idea occurred to him.

Maybe he could come up with a secret weapon. And maybe his secret weapon had just the thing one needed in order to run barefoot through fire . . . or to play Pilot football.

Quick feet.

Three

In St. Augustine, Seth had owned a 1988 Chevy Beretta. The car had a few rust spots, had been driven more than 150,000 miles and the front passenger door did not open from the inside. Still, Seth had loved the Beretta, mostly because it had been his first car.

A car his dad had helped him pick out.

When he and his mother had moved, Seth had been forced to get rid of the Beretta. "You can get something else when we get settled in Paavo," his mother had said. For now, however, he had no choice but to drive the mini-van.

Seth pulled the vehicle into the parking lot of what appeared to be a bowling alley. The reason it looked like a bowling alley was because this had been its original purpose. Years ago, however, it had closed and had sat empty for awhile. Then it had been remodeled and re-opened, but not as a bowling alley.

Running through fire, Seth thought while pulling the van alongside several much cooler cars.

A sign above the glass front door read Trean Gaoth Academy of Irish Dance.

Seth exited the mini-van and made his way inside. He found a wide, carpeted area littered with a few chairs where parents of young dancers sat and talked while lessons were in progress. Beyond this area stretched a broad, wooden dance floor, built over what had once been eight bowling lanes. A dozen or so small girls went through stretching exercises on this floor, led by an older woman in grubby black sweats. The area to Seth's left—which had probably once contained the bar—had been remodeled into several small offices.

Seth sought out the last office and knocked gently on the door jamb. Annie Delaney, the owner of Trean Gaoth Academy, whirled around in her desk chair, smiled and stood. Seth noticed that she was an inch or two taller than he was.

"Are you Seth?"

He nodded, stepped inside the office and shook her hand. Earlier in the day, Seth had placed a phone call to Trean Gaoth Academy and had spoken briefly to Annie. She appeared to be about thirty-five, with waves of golden hair tied back in a ponytail and penetrating green eyes behind smallish, oval eyeglasses. She wore navy-blue warm-up pants and a gold and navy-blue Trean Gaoth t-shirt.

"I'm glad you could stop by—and that you are interested in dancing. On the phone, you mentioned that you had dance experience?"

"I started seven years ago," he explained. "When we lived in Chicago."

Chicago seemed so distant that he might have been imagining someone else's life. His best friend had been Matt Parsons. Mrs. Parsons and Seth's mother had been good friends, too, and when Matt's two years younger sister begged for Irish dance lessons, the mothers had decided to sign up their nine-year-old sons, too.

"It'll get you away from the video games for an hour or two a week," Mrs. Parsons had chided her son.

Seth immediately decided that he would hate Irish dance and probably spend a good portion of the remainder of his life blaming his mother for the emotional scars that it had seared into his psyche. He had imagined that he would have to practice in pastel tights, prancing to the sort of music that might accompany butterflies in flight. Then, once a year, he and Matt would be forced to suffer the ultimate indignity: The Annual Recital. He would tromp around a stage in front of hundreds of parents who would recognize him for the uncoordinated buffoon he was.

To Seth's surprise, Irish dance had been nothing like that.

He practiced in the same sort of workout clothes he might have used to jog five miles. The pants and vest he wore for competition were jet black. The steps he learned were not only graceful and beautiful, but also powerful and precise and intense. Practices were as physically demanding as any sport he had ever attempted.

And while the Chicago dance group performed at several events during the year—spectacular, dynamic performances, Seth was forced to admit—there was another aspect of Irish dance that he hadn't expected: competition. He and Matt had traveled with their families to feiseanna—the Irish word for dance competitions—in Illinois, Iowa, Missouri, Indiana, Ohio and Wisconsin. Some featured more than two thousand dancers, though girls generally outnumbered the boys by a margin of about forty-to-one.

As Seth grew older, this disparity did not bother him so much.

He and Matt had started in the Beginner competition group, but moved into the higher Novice category as they accumulated awards. Eventually they moved up again, to the Open Prizewinner level. Seth had been on the verge of making another advancement when the family moved north.

"But you haven't danced recently?" continued Annie.

"We moved to northern Wisconsin a little more than two years ago," explained Seth. "There were no Irish dance schools."

"And now," continued Annie, paraphrasing their telephone conversation, "you want to get back into it?"

Seth nodded enthusiastically. "I really enjoyed it. Plus, I think it'll help my foot speed. For football."

Annie smiled. "What position do you play?"

Now Seth felt a bit self-conscious. "Quarterback, I guess."

Now Annie's eyes widened a bit. "Going to give Jason Troy a run for it?"

Seth was surprised. "You know Jason? Does he dance?"

Annie shook her head. "He doesn't dance. But in a small town like Paavo, everyone knows the quarterback of the high school team."

Seth tried to contain his startle. *Paavo? Small town? St. Augustine must be sub-atomic!*

"They say this might be Paavo's year," continued Annie.

"I guess," said Seth. "I just want to be a part of it. More than just a guy who sits on the bench."

Annie nodded knowingly. "And you think dance will help?"

Seth nodded.

She smiled and walked out into the building's main area. Seth followed. They stood watching the little girls go through their steps for a minute before Annie spoke.

"I guess the first thing to do is get an idea of where you're at. We want to put you in the right class. You're obviously not a beginner if you danced from age nine to age fourteen."

Seth thought of his first years in dance. Although he had joined at age nine, he had not started to compete until the following year.

"I was in Prizewinner," said Seth proudly. "Almost ready to move into PC."

Annie bowed her head slightly. "Very good. What dance would you like to do?"

Seth's eyes widened. "Right now?"

"Sure," said Annie matter-of-factly. "You haven't forgotten them, have you?"

Seth shook his head. "I guess I could do my hornpipe." As he slipped off his shoes, he began to hope he had not been lying about forgetting.

Annie knelt to cue up the appropriate music on a CD player near the wall. As it started, Seth came to attention, as rigid as a flagpole. After a few beats, he brought his right foot in front of the left in a point. As the melody recycled itself, he launched into his hornpipe steps.

Like riding a bicycle, he thought, as his feet flew through their steps, rapping out the complex choreography as if it were some frenetic Morse code. His arms remained glued to his sides, his eyes straight ahead. He noticed that the football training seemed to have had a beneficial effect: He felt less tired than usual as he worked his way to the left, then back to the right, leaping, kicking high, and finally finishing at the same instant the music concluded.

Annie clapped in approval. "You're quite a good dancer, Seth. Welcome to Trean Gaoth Academy!"

Seth thanked Annie and could not suppress a smile. However, a question now occurred to him.

"The name of the dance school, what's it mean?"

"It's Gaelic," Annie explained. "It means 'strong wind'."

Seth nodded and thought, *Perfect! Maybe a strong wind behind me is just what I need to get playing time on the football field!*

Four

School drew closer and so did the first game.

"This is our year, Pilots!" bellowed Coach Wisk as the team lurched through drills. Sweat streamed down their faces. The practice uniforms grew more tan than white. The first few days had been mostly about impressing the coaching staff. Now, as the team began its third week together, practices seemed more about merely surviving.

Still, Seth loved it. "When we're out there working hard, working together as a team, I sort of forget whether I'm at Paavo or at St. Augustine," he told Brandon as they sat together during a water break. "It feels good. It feels right." Although he never told anyone, the hard work also made him feel the way he had felt when his dad had been coaching him. He could almost pretend that his father was standing on the sidelines in his Osprey sweatshirt, whistle looped around his neck. He could almost feel him watching.

Brandon, on the other hand, seemed to wilt a bit more under the sun of each day's practice. One afternoon as they broke for water, Brandon rolled his eyes and dumped half a bottle of liquid onto his helmetless head. "It feels like I'm going right to the morgue. I think Coach Wisk's got it in for me. He's always making me do extra pushups and stuff."

"Maybe if you weren't such a slacker," said Seth, and in response, Brandon squirted the water bottle at him.

They dragged themselves back onto the practice field. As they ran sprints toward the end of the day, Coach Blair encouraged them from the fourth row of the bleachers. "This Friday's our first test, boys! Who's ready?"

A chorus of "Me" seemed to shake the very air.

"Well I've got news for all of you," grunted Coach Wisk. "You mushrooms ain't ready to win a pickup game against a all-girls pre-school! If I have to run you all afternoon, I'll do it, until I see good effort from everyone!"

When the practice ended, Seth crawled over to where Brandon lay on his back.

"I made it up to sprint group two!" Seth told his panting friend. "I'm almost there!"

Brandon poured water onto his face and closed his eyes. "I'm almost there, too. I see a bright light. And my great grandpa. And my Aunt Linda. And the two goldfish that we flushed down the toilet when I was five. I'm coming Goldie! I'm coming Firetruck!"

"You named a goldfish Firetruck?"

"I was five!"

Seth propped himself on an elbow to assess his friend's condition. "Is there anything I can do for you?"

"Pull the plug? Cyanide? Hey, tell that cute sophomore cheerleader, Marcie, that I mentioned her right before I crossed over."

Seth smiled. "If you can joke around, I know you're not dying."

"Who says I'm joking?" But now, Brandon propped himself up, too. Other football players sat in heaps on the edge of the practice field. "It's like a Civil War hospital. Like in *Gone with the Wind*."

Seth noticed now that not all of his teammates appeared to be mortally wounded. Jason, for instance, had found his feet and was walking toward the bleachers—toward a slender girl with long, blonde hair. She wore shorts, a red tank top and a wide smile.

"Stop drooling," said Brandon, noticing the direction Seth was staring. "In this heat, you'll get dehydrated. That's Troy's girlfriend, Mallory Lyons. As incredible as it may seem, yes, she *is* a cheerleader."

"I wasn't drooling," said Seth, checking the front of his practice jersey. "Was I?"

Brandon sat up all the way now, a sure sign that he would recover. "Don't worry. If you're a Pilot football player, you'll have girls interested in you. They'll even be interested in me. We just won't get the top of the line stuff, like the starting quarterback gets."

"I don't think I've even met a girl since I arrived in Paavo," noted Seth.

"Wait until school starts next week," advised Brandon. "The first time you wear your Pilots jersey to school, you'll get all kinds of looks."

The two showered and headed for Brandon's pickup truck, feeling only marginally refreshed. "Why don't you come over to my house for lunch?" asked Brandon. "We can hang out there playing video games until next practice at five."

Seth used his phone to check in with his mother, and then the two boys headed for Brandon's. This was Seth's first trip to his friend's house, which turned out to be a nice-looking, tan, ranch-style home in a subdivision half a mile from Paavo High School.

"Sandwich or pizza?" asked Brandon as the two boys burst into the kitchen.

"Either," said Seth. "I'm starved."

Brandon nodded, opening the doors to the refrigerator and freezer simultaneously. "Sounds like both." He removed a frozen pizza, a loaf of bread, lunch meat, cheese, mayo and butter. In a moment, he had popped the pizza into the oven and was busy laying out bread slices.

Seth stepped up to the counter. "I can help."

In a few minutes, the boys carried their finished creations to the small kitchen table and settled in. Then Brandon popped back to his feet. "Drinks!"

"Yeah, I'm still dying. What do you have?"

Brandon swung the refrigerator door wide and peered inside. "Milk. Lemonade. Orange juice. There's a green tea here, too."

"I'll take the green tea," said Seth.

Brandon returned with the drinks and the boys tore into their sandwiches. After a few minutes, Seth heard the soft pad of bare feet on the floor and a girl who appeared to be a year or so younger than Brandon entered the kitchen. He acknowledged her by pointing a thumb and, with a full mouth, grunted, "My sister."

The girl wore baggy gray pants, a loose-fitting wrinkled brown t-shirt and her unkempt dishwater hair hung in front of almost half her face. She stopped at the counter where the boys had conducted their assembly line and had left the bread bag open, the lunch meat sitting out and various knives and spoons soiled.

"You'd better be planning to clean up this mess, because I'm not going to do it!"

Brandon offered a dismissive wave with a hand. "Don't worry about it, Kimmy."

Kimmy gave her brother a snarl, and turned to the refrigerator. After rummaging in it a moment, she jerked back toward the table."

"Where's my green tea?"

Seth stopped chewing.

Brandon motioned to his friend. "Seth's our lunch guest. He wanted it."

Kimmy spotted the half-finished bottle of green tea on the table and gave a look which, though only half visible due to the mop of dangling hair, seemed twice as nasty as the one she had given her brother.

"Jerk!" she cried to Seth, and then stomped bare-footedly out of the room.

Brandon watched her go and then turned back to his friend. "Congratulations! Now you've met a girl from Paavo!"

Five

The music carried him like a strong wind, his feet flying across the wooden floor with percussive intricacy, like fingers skipping purposefully across a piano keyboard or the crackle of thunder ending a summer storm. Seth loved the hard shoe dances. The bullet-rhythm of his feet seemed to connect him physically with the music. The turns, the leaps, the kicks demanded an athleticism that was every bit as challenging as football—yet different.

"Good, good," called Annie, moving slowly at the edge of the practice floor, her eyes carefully traveling from dancer to dancer. Fifteen boys and girls attended Seth's Wednesday night class, ranging in age from eight to seventeen. Two thirds of them were PC or Provisional Champion level dancers, while the others—including Seth—were in Open Prizewinner.

When the fifteen danced, their feet slammed into the floor like one great ax splitting hardwood. It reminded Seth of *Isle of Green Fire*, the Irish musical his parents had taken him to see in Chicago when they had lived there. Their feet finished, delivering one monumental blast, and then the fifteen bowed.

"I don't know how you can handle the first day of school, football and dance all in one twelve-hour period," Brandon had said after practice. "I can hardly move my arms. I think my mom's going to have to feed me through an IV tube!"

Seth had been having no trouble handling both football and dance practices. The first day of school had been dull, but not physically taxing. Somehow, passing out textbooks and going over classroom rules—which should have taken about eight minutes—had dragged on for eight hours.

Football actually energized Seth on most days. It meant drilling, running sprints and mastering the playbook. Mostly, it meant repetition. "We'll do it until we get it right!" was one of Coach Wisk's favorite sayings.

Dance practice, on the other hand, meant stretching, drills and mastering the new steps that Annie taught him. "As you know, every dance school has its own unique choreography for the basic dances," she told him. "However, the core steps are similar, and as advanced as you are, you should pick up our routines in no time."

As they sat on the dance floor stretching after practice, Annie went from dancer to dancer, offering words of advice, encouragement or simple small talk.

When she came to Seth, she knelt down. "Looks like I was right about you catching on to those new steps."

Seth smiled. "I think it's helping my foot speed. In football, I moved up to the second sprint group."

Annie smiled and stood up. "Just don't let anybody bust those knees of yours."

As Seth pulled off his shoes at the end of practice, Shelby, a short-haired blonde girl, called over to him. "Did I hear you say you're on the football team?"

Seth nodded. "It's pretty cool." He thought this answer sounded pretty lame, but he hoped Shelby would not notice.

She seemed to appraise him for a moment. "You're new, right? How long have you danced?"

Seth explained the moves from Chicago to northern Wisconsin to Paavo.

"Well, good luck," said Shelby as he finished. "Maybe I'll see you at school."

She left the dance floor and Seth finished putting on his street shoes. Then he headed out to the van.

Okay, he thought. *Now I've met two girls since I got to Paavo. And one of them seems pretty nice.*

By the time Seth got home, it was almost nine. He was physically tired from football practice. And dance practice. Yet, he had trouble falling immediately asleep.

The first game of the season was only two days away.

And he had met a girl.

Friday night's game against Drumlin provided the biggest distraction. He felt nervous already. Not because he would play much. Being the third-string quarterback, he figured he would be glued to a spot on the bench for the entire game. Nonetheless, simply being a part of the team—a powerful juggernaut that had captured the imagination of the entire community—why, that was enough to make anyone a little nervous. Even though today had been the first day of school, the game had seemed to be the hot topic of student discussion. Half of Seth's teachers had even managed to work it into the discussion somehow.

He finally crawled into bed a few minutes after eleven.

Thursday, classes seemed to drag even more than when the teachers had been lecturing about rules the previous day. Brandon told him that's the way it always was the day before a game. When the bell finally sounded at the end of the day, Seth felt relieved. When he got to the locker room, however, he found a surprise.

An unpleasant surprise.

A sign had been taped to his locker. It featured a crude caricature of a dancer in pink tights. Large letters above the picture spelled out TWINKLETOES.

As other members of the team filed in, some began to laugh loudly and repeated the name.

"Hey, Twinkletoes!"

"What's up, Twink?"

"Yo, Twink, lookin' good!"

How had they discovered that he was a dancer? He had told Brandon and no one else. Had someone seen him going into Trean Gaoth Academy?

Then he remembered Shelby.

Seth tore down the sign and, red-faced, began to put on his practice gear.

Maybe there are no nice girls in Paavo.

The jeers continued.

"Hey, Twink! Why don't you ditch that jockstrap and get yourself a kilt?"

"You know, real men only dance in the end zone! Not that you'll ever get that opportunity!"

"Dance like a leprechaun for us, Twink!"

This idea seemed to appeal to several and they began a chant:

"Twink! Twink! Twink! Twink!"

Danny performed a vulgar version of the Mexican hat dance in front of the bench where Seth sat as the chant continued.

Then, with a terrifying suddenness, the chant stopped and Coach Blair stood in the room. His voice was terrifying with its quiet calmness.

"This doesn't look like a team that's focused. This doesn't look like a team that's unified. Our job is to beat Friday night's opponent, not each other."

So that none of them would forget, Coach Wisk had everyone run extra laps of the football field after practice.

Brandon drew deep, pained breaths as he jogged next to Seth, barely managing to choke out his thoughts. "I hope this Irish dancing stuff turns out to be worth all the abuse."

Seth said nothing. But he hoped so, too.

Six

Everybody seemed to be talking about the first game of the season, the game that would put the Paavo Pilots on their way toward an eventual state championship.

"Isn't it great?" said Brandon as he and Seth strode down the hallway toward English class. "On game days, we all wear our football jerseys and it's like we're superheroes or something."

Seth had to admit that it was true. Girls he had never met smiled at him when they saw the green and white Paavo jersey with the number "8" and his last name across the shoulders in back. And almost every teacher had waved or winked and offered a "Good luck!"

All the same, every time he received a smile or shout of encouragement, he felt a twinge of frustration. If he wore an Irish dance t-shirt to school, he knew that no one would wish him well. If the reaction of the football team served as any indication, he would probably be ridiculed.

At lunch, the football players all sat at a group of tables that had been pushed together, forming a pulsing green and white mass in the middle of the cafeteria. Brandon waved his toasted cheese sandwich in the air as he spoke from his seat across the table.

"Someone said they're sending out a news helicopter from Milwaukee to cover the game. I'm so excited I've had to ask for a bathroom pass in every class!"

Seth laughed and wiped a dribble of tomato soup from his chin. "I'll bet we kill Drumlin by thirty points."

Now Brandon grew more serious. "You heard what Coach Blair said. 'On any given day, any team can beat any other team. Records are meaningless.'"

"But all coaches say that. It's so you don't take anything for granted."

Brandon nodded. "True. But Coach Wisk says Drumlin is a scary team."

Seth paused with a plastic spoonful of soup halfway to his mouth. "Scary?"

"Drumlin finished with six wins and five losses last year," reported Brandon.

Seth shrugged. "But Paavo had nine wins."

"Right," admitted Brandon, "but Drumlin has a new running back this year. Real speedy guy by the name of LaForte. Moved out here from Milwaukee, I guess. Someone said he finished third at the state track meet in the 100-meter dash."

"That does sound scary," Seth conceded. "Hope I don't have to chase him down tonight."

"There's more," interrupted Brandon. "Last year, Drumlin just squeaked into the playoffs with a 5-4 regular-season record. But then in the playoffs, they upset unbeaten Rock River before losing in the second round!"

"That's scary, too."

"It gets scarier. One of Drumlin's five regular season wins was against us!"

Seth blinked. "They beat Paavo? But I thought we were so good last year!"

Brandon met Seth's gaze and nodded. "On any given day . . ."

All week long, Seth had been imagining that Paavo would roll over the first opponent like an armored tank. It seemed everyone on the team and the entire population of the school felt this way, too. He remembered Coach Blair and Coach Wisk telling them all not to take the game lightly, that Drumlin was a good team, and that they had some excellent players back from last year's squad. However, it seemed like he and all of the other players had ignored it, like when parents tell kids to make sure to wear sunscreen at summer camp.

A crashing sound shook Seth out of his sobering reflections. He turned—as did everyone in the lunch room—and saw that a boy in the food line had dropped his tray, creating a mess of sound, peach slices and sandwich fragments.

A cheer went up from the football table, and Seth's teammates began a chant.

Squirrel chasers! Squirrel chasers! Squirrel chasers!

Noticing his friend's confusion, Brandon pointed. "That kid's on the cross country team."

As the thin boy stood with food scraps in his hands, looking for the trash receptacle, Seth noticed his green and white Pilots cross country jersey. He figured they must have a meet tonight, or the next day.

"We call cross country runners squirrel chasers!" Brandon explained.

The loud chanting continued and Seth found himself pulled into it.

"Squirrel chasers! Squirrel chasers!"

The thin boy seemed to grow redder by the moment. The chanting grew louder. It felt good to not be the target, to be joining in with his teammates to dish it out to someone else.

But then he recalled how he had felt when he had first seen the "TWINKLETOES" sign on his locker and he turned his attention back to his grilled cheese sandwich.

Seven

The eighty members of the Paavo Pilots varsity football team sat in the gymnasium in full game uniforms, their helmets in their laps. No one said a word. They all stared at an old football, dark-brown and worn smooth, a ball that had been placed on the wooden gymnasium floor.

Brandon had explained that this was the Bobby Farrell ball.

Fifty years earlier, Farrell had carried that ball for 121 yards and two touchdowns to lead the Pilots to a 14-10 win over Rock River. Although there were no state playoffs at the time, the game had been widely recognized as a contest between the two best football teams in Wisconsin. Ever since Coach Blair had taken over the Paavo team twenty-five years ago, he retrieved the Bobby Farrell ball from its nest in the trophy case before every game, sitting it on the gym floor in front of his team. They would then focus on the ball for twenty minutes, collecting their thoughts, getting into the proper frame of mind to play Pilot football.

Then, as he did now, Coach Blair would step in front and address the team.

"Men, the first game is always important. It sets the tone for the season ahead. And we've got a big season planned. Now let's go out there and show that home crowd what sort of football team they've got this year!"

This was the cue for Jason, the team captain, who stood up and began the chant. "Pilots! Pilots!"

The rest immediately joined in, and the noise seemed to shake the steel rafters.

Then the school song boomed over the gymnasium's public address system and Jason led the team outside. Seth felt more ready than he had ever felt before a St. Augustine game, almost ready to chase down the speedy Drumlin running back LaForte by himself if he had to.

The Paavo stadium was similar to the field he had played on in St. Augustine. A 400-meter running track circled the football field. Bleachers lined the far side of the field, which was lit by powerful floodlights on six tall poles. However, the crowd for tiny St. Augustine's games had numbered in the hundreds. Seth was certain there were several thousand people in the stands for this game.

The noise the crowd made when the Pilots took the field sounded more like a million.

Jason led the team around the north goalpost, and then they gathered in a huge circle for warm-up exercises. After that, they broke into groups for more specific preparation. As Seth played catch with a third-string tight end, he took in the excitement and spectacle. The cheerleaders were busy pumping up the crowd. The pep band occasionally broke into a spirited fight song. On the far end of the field, Drumlin's red jerseys moved in their own kind of warm-up ballet. Jason Troy's voice boomed above all the background noise as he barked out signals to the first-string Paavo offense.

Dad would be standing right at the end of the bench, thought Seth. Then he squinted across the field to where the parents of most of the Paavo players sat. His mother would be somewhere in the crowd. *You'll have to cheer loud enough for two, ma.*

Before Seth could pull his eyes away from the blur of humanity, he recognized a face among the cheerleaders.

It's that girl from dance. Shelby. The girl who told them about me. As she spun toward the field, Seth lowered his eyes and turned to face the rest of the team.

In no time at all, Coach Blair got the boys together for a final spirit cheer, and Jason jogged back from center field where he reported that Drumlin had won the toss and would receive the kick.

On the first series, the Pilot defense rose to the occasion. LaForte, who looked every bit as fast as

Brandon had warned, gained seven yards on his first carry. But then the Drumlin quarterback was dropped for a four-yard loss on second down. When his third-down pass fell incomplete, Drumlin was forced to punt.

Paavo got the ball on its own nineteen yard line and Jason jogged confidently out to command his troops. From the first play, Seth could see why everyone spoke so highly of Jason. He moved fluidly behind his solid front line, sometimes handing to a back, sometimes dishing a short pass to a tight end or wide out. Paavo moved the ball past mid-field, inching closer to the goal line.

"They can't stop us!" said Brandon excitedly from his seat on the bench beside Seth.

As if to underscore this notion, the announcer's voice boomed out over the public address system. "There's another four yards for Anderson. It's first down for Paavo at the Drumlin sixteen yard line!"

On any given day, thought Seth. This did not look like it was Drumlin's given day.

Jason took the snap from center on first down, but something happened as he tried to hand off to Anderson and the ball ended up on the ground. Everyone on the sidelines jumped to their feet. After a short scramble, a cheer erupted from the Drumlin bench.

"Drumlin recovers the fumble," confirmed the announcer disconsolately.

Seth and his teammates groaned.

"We'll get it back," said Brandon confidently. "We're completely controlling the line of scrimmage."

Seth nodded and looked back toward the field just in time to see LaForte take a handoff and sweep around the right side. He cut back, leaving one Paavo player grasping at air. He sliced in the other direction, and a second Paavo player missed an arm tackle. Then LaForte accelerated like a rocket between two defenders and suddenly there was no one between him and the goal line.

"Touchdown, Drumlin," said the announcer with a sort of forlorn enthusiasm.

Some of the energy seemed to have drained from the stadium.

Brandon clapped his hands. "We'll get it back!"

He was right. Jason engineered a brilliant drive in the second quarter, which gave the pilots a touchdown. Then in the third quarter he led the team to the twenty where Danny Sidowski kicked a field goal. Another touchdown gave the Pilots a 17-14 advantage with three minutes to play.

Seth noticed that his friend was now so nervous he had stopped making optimistic predictions. "I'll just be glad when this game is over. We're lucky LaForte has butterfingers."

The star Drumlin running back had scored both of his team's touchdowns and had rolled up more than 180 yards. However, he had fumbled twice inside the Paavo twenty, and the Drumlin quarterback had thrown an interception to end another scoring drive.

Drumlin got the ball back on its own twenty-six yard line.

"No way they can drive seventy-four yards in only three minutes," said Brandon, pacing back and forth like a death row prisoner. "Is there?"

Seth said nothing. He simply watched as LaForte began chipping away at the Paavo defense, three yards here, four there, a sudden burst for nine. Then the Pilots began to take chances, sending two, three, even five players after LaForte on each snap. With six seconds left, Drumlin called time out, stuck on the Paavo twenty-eight yard line.

"No way will they try a field goal," crowed Brandon. "Their kicker doesn't have a strong-enough leg. It was close, but we've got them!"

Seth still said nothing. When Drumlin lined up, every player and fan in the stadium was standing, and the roar sounded like a freight train.

It surprised no one when the Drumlin quarterback pitched the ball to LaForte. He was their money player. Most of the Paavo team had sniffed out the play and were closing on his side of the field. Then, instead of turning the corner and heading into the mass of Paavo players that stood between him and the end zone, LaForte handed off to a teammate who had lined up wide and was now powering back in the opposite direction.

Brandon looked ready to claw out of his skin. "Reverse! It's a reverse!"

The Pilot defense had gambled, and the result was a wide-open field behind LaForte. Paavo fans could only watch in helpless horror as the Drumlin speedster loped into the end zone untouched—with no time left on the clock.

A dispirited "Touchdown, Drumlin" tolled over the public address system.

Brandon, his face ashen, put a heavy hand on Seth's shoulder. "Don't worry, buddy. In a minute, I'll wake up and this nightmare will be gone."

Before Seth could respond, he and Brandon were shoved violently aside. Seth turned to see Jason elbowing his way though the crowd of disappointed players.

"Stupid defense!" Jason bellowed. "Lost the game for us!"

He threw a forearm into a table filled with water filled cups as he passed and sent them flying.

Brandon looked at Seth. "This isn't a dream, is it?"

The two boys had planned on stopping at The Hangar for victory fries and shakes after the game, but the stunning outcome had left them in no mood to socialize.

"If I had a contented look on my face for half a second because the fries were good, I'd feel guilty," said Brandon as they exited the locker room. "After a loss like this, we deserve to be miserable. So I think

I'll go home and listen to music from Kimmy's collection."

"Oldies?" guessed Seth.

"Worse," said Brandon. "Show tunes. Maybe I'll fall asleep listening to something from *Cats*."

He dropped Seth in front of the Kerrighan home, although Seth still did not find it very homey. The bungalow with an open front porch and UPS-brown siding seemed dark and tiny compared to the white Victorian-style home they had owned in St. Augustine. It was also missing the light that his father had always brought to the family.

The kitchen clock read quarter to ten as Seth dropped his duffel onto the table. Aside from the light over the sink, the rest of the house seemed dark.

"Ma?"

He heard muffled sounds from the living room and moved through the kitchen to it as a light came on. His mother had one hand on a table lamp, propping herself up on the couch with the other. A light throw covered her legs.

"You're home," said Mrs. Kerrighan.

"Just got," said Seth, sensing that something was wrong with the picture. His mother's next question confirmed his suspicion.

"How was the game?"

Seth felt something heavy drop into the nether regions of his gut. "Weren't you at the game, Ma?"

Mrs. Kerrighan rubbed the back of a hand over her eyes. She was small, thin with dark, tired eyes.

Her light brown hair had been pulled back into a knot, and despite the fact that she had apparently been asleep, she looked exhausted. "No, honey. I stayed home."

Stayed home? Seth had never felt so overwhelmingly disappointed, although anger also swept through him in a wave. "We lost the game."

"Oh, Seth, I'm sorry. Your first game here."

"My first game here," echoed Seth. "But you didn't come to see it."

She sat up fully now. "You didn't need me there."

Need her there? Of course he needed her there. She was all he had now. His father had always been on the sidelines. He had assumed his mother would be watching tonight. She had told him she would be there.

"I changed my mind," she said simply.

Seth almost laughed, but his tone was bitter. "How could you change your mind? It's not like you had some important appointment or were out of town. You know how important football is to me, and you just sat at home on the couch, sleeping!"

"Seth, I couldn't." He noticed the sadness in her face, of course. Knew he should stop arguing the issue. But he couldn't. He was hurt. And he was a teenager.

"You couldn't? If you'd had a broken leg, maybe you couldn't. If the car broke down, maybe then you couldn't. But it wasn't like that, was it?"

"Seth," said his mother quietly, "I miss your father."

This stopped him. He stood there, staring at her on the sofa, staring at her smallness, her vulnerability.

"Football was so important to him," she continued.

"It is to me, too," said Seth.

"If I had gone to that game, I would have been alone in the crowd. I don't know anyone here. None of the other mothers."

"You'd get to know them," said Seth in rebuttal.

"I'd be alone there, staring at the place at the end of the bench where you father used to always be. Waiting to hear him shout your name. Looking to see him put his arm around your shoulders at the end of the game as you came up into the stands to me. But he's not there, Seth. Not at the end of the bench, not at the end of the game. And I can't face that yet."

He understood completely. That was the problem. He understood completely, yet could not bring himself to do what he should have done. He knew he should go to his mother, sit beside her, put his arm around her.

And tell her that he understood.

Instead he turned and trudged up the stairs to his room.

Eight

Saturdays had recently become busier than school days. The coaching staff required pilot football players to be at the high school every Saturday at eight in the morning to watch films of the previous night's game.

"I think Coach Wisk started yelling about thirty seconds into the film and didn't stop until right before the last play of the game," said Seth as he and Brandon walked to the weight room afterwards.

"I believe Coach Wisk added at least seven or eight words to my vocabulary," said Brandon. "Though I won't be able to use any of them on a vocabulary test. Or around home. Or ever."

The two boys began their lifting routine, which included sets with light weights at various stations followed by stretching in between.

"At least Coach Blair didn't scream at us," noted Brandon as he slipped metal disks onto the bar.

Seth finished a set of curls. "In some ways, I wish he would. He just speaks quietly, like he's disappointed in us. It makes me feel terrible." Seth had felt terrible long before Blair had begun speaking. When he woke, he immediately remembered the previous evening's conversation with his mother. He had thought he might apologize, but when he peaked in at her bedroom door, he saw that she was still sleeping.

She seemed to sleep a lot since they had moved to Paavo.

Blair had reminded them that the first game of the season did not necessarily determine where they would finish in the standings. "I truly feel we should have beaten Drumlin. We made some mistakes, and we're going to work hard to make sure we don't repeat them. But Drumlin is a good team, and if we play well the rest of the season, we may get another crack at them in the playoffs!"

As Seth grabbed a jump rope and began his two hundred reps, he thought about the long season ahead. Eight games remained before the playoffs. He certainly did not want to spend that two-month span sitting on the bench for three hours every Friday night.

He jumped faster.

Seth also did not relish a repeat of the "Twinkletoes" episode. No one had ever done anything like that in St. Augustine. Of course, he had not been taking dance classes when his family had lived in northern Wisconsin. *The guys at St. Augustine would have been cool with my dancing,* Seth told himself.

Or was this simply the way he wanted to remember his former home, a fiction he had created to make himself feel better? Perhaps teenagers really were not much different regardless of the size of their schools.

Brandon seemed to have no problem with Irish dancing.

"You've got the fastest feet I've ever seen," he had told Seth, his voice filled with admiration. "If my feet were that fast, I'd always be the first one in line in the cafeteria for chicken chunk Thursday!"

At dance practice the following week, Seth spoke to Annie about what had happened in the locker room.

"What am I supposed to do when people make fun of me?"

Annie sighed. "I'd tell you to ignore them, but you're looking for something else, aren't you?"

Seth nodded.

Annie smiled. "Is it the whole team that is teasing you?"

"Pretty much."

"Really?"

Seth thought about it. "My friend Brandon doesn't. He thinks my feet are rockets." He tried to remember that day in the locker room. Only a couple of players had actually said anything nasty to him. And when the chanting had started, it seemed to him that half of the players continued to go about their business, showering, dressing, combing their hair. Maybe more than half.

"Maybe it's not the whole team, but it still hurts."

"One of my teachers in high school gave me this advice," said Annie. "He used to say, 'the best revenge is to live a good life'."

Lines appeared on Seth's forehead. "I'm not sure what that's supposed to mean."

Annie explained. "Don't sink to their level. If you try to say or do mean things to the people who have treated you badly, it makes them feel like they were right to hurt you. Being successful is the best way to respond. If Irish dance helps you to be a better player, if it helps you to succeed, that will be your answer to them."

"So you think Irish dance will make me a better football player than Jason Troy?"

"If your hard work and your dance practice makes you a better football player, one of two things will happen," said Annie. "Either you'll pass up Jason Troy and become the Pilots' starting quarterback, or Jason will have to work harder and get better to keep his spot. Either way, it will be a good thing for your team, and I'll bet your improvement will earn their respect."

Nine

The Pilots beat Waterville High in game two, but it took two fourth-quarter touchdowns—one to go ahead, and a second to settle the issue.

Seth and Brandon again watched from the bench.

"Don't worry," said Brandon. "We'll have a couple of blowouts before the year's over. Then coach'll put us in."

Seth smiled at his friend to show his appreciation. However, he had no real interest in being a member of the "blowout squad". Seth wanted to see real action when the game still hung in the balance.

"Pigs will fly, pop stars will stop getting tattoos, and parents will forget to give out curfews before that will happen," said Brandon.

Airborne hams aside, Seth's friend seemed to be devoting less mental energy to football lately, and more to a different "game": getting a date for the Homecoming dance.

"Because we're members of the varsity football team, it's almost a law that girls have to say yes if we ask them to the dance," said Brandon, his eyes glassy.

"Would you really want to go out with a girl who's only with you because of which sport you belong to?" asked Seth.

"Yes!" cried Brandon.

"Wouldn't you rather have someone who thinks you're interesting, who cares about how you're feeling?"

"But we're not interesting!" argued Brandon. "We're two bench-warming high school juniors who have no useful skills or informed opinions about anything! And no one cares how you're feeling. This is high school, not group therapy at the state prison."

Despite Brandon's cynicism, Seth still wanted to go to the dance. However, he had met only a few girls so far, and none seemed like good candidates for Homecoming dates, unless one was looking to date a terrorist. Brandon's sister, Kimmy, seemed perpetually angry. Shelby, the snobbish back-stabber, had leaked information about Seth's dancing to the football team. He knew another girl from physics class, but she had a boyfriend. And there was a girl from the cross country team that he had talked to a couple of times, but that had fizzled.

"Dude, are you mental or what?" Brandon cried when Seth explained this to his friend. "You have the best setup of all! You're an Irish dancer! You told me that the girls outnumber the boys by a ratio of like forty to one. Forty to one! Man, a cadaver could get a date with those odds!"

Seth had of course considered this favorable ratio before, but never with an actual event like Homecoming as a catalyst to propel him toward action. "I've got a feis coming up this Saturday."

Brandon wrinkled his nose. "What the heck's a feis?"

"It's an Irish dance competition."

Brandon snorted. "Competition? What do you do, dance against some other guy in a kilt until one of you gets exhausted and collapses?"

"Pretty much," said Seth. "Except we also get to kick-box each other with our razor-tipped dance shoes."

Brandon's mouth fell open. "Really?"

Seth rolled his eyes. "No, you idiot! All the competitors line up along the back of a thirty-foot stage facing a judge. Two come out to the center at a time. They dance to live music for about two minutes. They try to get their kicks high, keep the toes pointed, move the feet fast, stay with the music. Then two more come out and dance. The judge decides who's the best."

"No razor-toed kick-boxing?"

Seth shook his head.

A worried look suddenly appeared on Brandon's face. "You can't dance at a feis on Saturday! We've got game film and weight training!"

"My age group doesn't dance until later in the day, and it's not a long drive. Lake Forest."

Brandon considered this new information. "Take me with you!"

On Saturday, the team review of the game film took half an hour less than usual. In the previous night's game against West Lapham High, Paavo won easily: 31-0. Jason Troy threw for three touchdowns. Even Coach Wisk was in a good mood, and as a result, he said little during the film, which meant they finished early. Then after weight training, Seth and Brandon headed off to Lake Forest.

"This is going to be great," said Brandon as the two hurried out of the locker room.

Seth nodded in agreement. "Feiseanna are really very colorful. Lots of different costumes. And the competition, especially at the higher levels, is really awesome."

Brandon rolled his eyes. "I meant all those girls in one place!" He wore his Paavo Pilots football jersey, which he informed Seth was a sure ticket to attracting the attention of the ladies.

"But," argued Seth, "half of these girls will be from some other state. They won't even have heard of Paavo football!"

Brandon's eyes glazed, unable to process this notion.

"And," continued Seth, "no girl from Indiana or Missouri is going to want to travel three hundred miles to go to a Homecoming dance at Paavo."

Brandon's enthusiasm remained undiminished. "You said there will be 1,400 girls at this feis, right?"

Seth nodded.

Brandon smiled. "Then I'd say the odds are still in my favor."

He felt pretty good on the drive to Lake Forest. Seth was nervous, of course, as he always was before a feis. Probably more so this time because he had not danced in competition for such a long interval. However, he was anxious to get back on the stage, to feel the energy that he always drew from dance. This would also be his first feis without a parent by his side. He had reached a kind of truce with his mother about her avoidance of football games. However, he was not anxious for another argument, and so he had not pressed her about coming to the feis.

Naturally, Seth also felt good because his football team had won big the previous night. The fans had roared and everybody had traded high fives and helmet butts. Yet, he felt a bit uneasy, even disappointed, about one aspect of the game. He and Brandon had remained on the bench.

"Just how many points do we have to be winning by in order for coach to put us in?" Seth had asked Brandon at the Hangar as they chowed on burgers and fries after the game. "Thirty-one to zero seems like a blowout to me."

"I heard some of the guys talking," explained Brandon. "Blair was going to put us in, but Wisk talked him out of it."

Seth's eyes widened. "Why would he do that?"

"The way I heard it," continued Brandon, "was that Wisk wanted to make a statement. To show the town and other teams in the conference that we're studs."

"That stinks!" said Seth, his eyes dark, focused on an empty spot on the tabletop.

Brandon attempted to console him. "Don't worry. Next time we're ahead by thirty, we'll get in. We just needed this big game for our morale!"

Seth took a sip from his chocolate shake. "It didn't do much for *my* morale. I don't want to wait for the next time we're ahead by thirty!"

The shake suddenly did not satisfy him at all, and he tossed it toward the garbage receptacle across from their table—a little too hard. Instead of bouncing into the round hole, it hit the smooth backstop and the plastic lid popped off, splattering chocolate shake on the wall and the top of the trash receptacle. Seth's mouth fell open and he gasped, but Brandon began to laugh. "Sweet!"

A girl in a green and white striped Hangar t-shirt arrived with a bucket and sponge and began cleaning the mess.

Seth stood and fumbled for words. "I-I'm sorry. I didn't mean to—"

He stopped as the girl turned toward him.

Brandon's sister, Kimmy.

The dark in her eyes radiated Black Hole Status to the tenth power. When she spoke, however, it was almost in a whisper.

"Nice job, Mr. Quarterback. With a touch like that, I can see why you're not starting."

She finished quickly and walked away.

Brandon slapped him on the shoulder. "Beautiful! Man, I owe you!"

Seth glowered at his friend. "Your sister works here?"

Brandon nodded gleefully. "Isn't it the best? She hates football, and this is where all the football players meet after games and practices. And what you just did, splooshing that shake, and then my sister having to clean it up, wow, priceless! I couldn't have written a better script if I were Quentin Tarantino and I had included a lot more blood! And razor-toed kick-boxing!"

He pulled into the parking lot, grabbed his garment and shoe bags from the backseat and headed for the main entrance of the hotel where the feis was being held. Brandon followed, yammering incessantly about the anticipated forty-to-one gender ratio happily stacked against him.

Inside, there were medals to be won. There were girls who might want to go to Paavo's Homecoming dance with him.

He was off the bench and into the game.

"Good luck!" called Brandon as they approached the main entrance.

Seth turned to his friend. "I might be a little rusty. I haven't competed in a couple of years."

"I meant finding a date!" called Brandon, and then the two disappeared into the hotel.

Ten

The hotel was like the inside of an anthill—if the ants had thought to line the floors of their tunnels with plush, Oriental-style carpeting, their walls with ornate gold-and-crystal light fixtures, and their ant gift shops with $7 bottles of soda pop. The activity level, however, was precisely the same. People moved purposefully, some proceeding down a long hallway toward banquet rooms where the dance stages most likely had been erected, some heading to a bank of elevators along the far wall, others rushing to a series of tables set up in a wide reception area adjacent to the lobby for feis registration. This was where Seth headed.

He picked up his competitor number, glanced at the map printed inside the feis program, and then steered Brandon down the hallway toward "The Lakeshore Ballroom". Since they were arriving several hours after the start of the feis, the competition was in full bustle. Dancers and parents hurried in all directions. Crowds gathered in front of the vendors set up along one side of the wide hallway, offering feis t-shirts, Irish jewelry, Celtic music and even books. In the ballroom, hundreds of people had spread blankets near the back wall like a mass picnic. Collapsible chairs had been erected on some of these. Dancers sat applying makeup or adjusting their costumes. Parents read books or napped. Several plywood dance stages had been erected along the perimeter of the ballroom, each with rows of folding chairs to hold spectators and dancers. A musician—often a fiddler or accordion player—sat at a corner of each stage while a judge presided over each venue from a table in front.

Brandon's mouth hung open. "There must be a thousand people in here! This isn't how I imagined it at all!"

Seth smiled as he found a tiny open spot on the carpet to set his things. "How did you imagine it?"

"I don't know," grumbled Brandon. "Like a bunch of nerdy kids dancing to a bad recording of bagpipe music. But it's not like that. This is kind of awesome."

Seth squinted in the direction of stage number three. He took a few steps toward it and then quickly returned. "It looks like there are still a few groups that are scheduled to perform before mine comes up. I'd say maybe half an hour." With that, he unzipped his garment bag and pulled out a wine-red shirt on a hangar. He already wore his black performance pants, and now buttoned the shirt over his PILOT FOOTBALL t-shirt.

Brandon pointed to another boy dancer. "He's wearing a blue shirt. Is that significant? Is it like belt colors in karate?"

Seth laughed. "Dancers start out in Beginner One wearing a plain school costume. When they place high enough in their required dances, they move to Beginner Two. Then into Novice. When a dancer earns a first place in novice, he earns his solo shirt. You can wear a vest, too." Seth held his up, and then slipped his arms into it.

Brandon helped with Seth's tie, glossy black with red polka-dots.

The last time he had danced in competition, his father had tied the knot.

After dispatching the tie, Seth laced on his dance shoes, following up with a meticulous inspection and touch-up with the lint brush.

"It's like in King Arthur's days," said Brandon, "when knights put on their armor and readied for battle. Only with less blood."

"Wait until you see the blisters on my feet afterwards," warned Seth.

The anticipated half hour passed. Then another half hour. Finally, Seth's group checked in with the stage monitor and the five competitors lined up along the back of the stage. Seth and a boy from an Ohio dance school stepped to center. The music began, and Seth's toe came to point. Moments later he swept across the stage—powerfully, gracefully, full of energy and joy.

"You were amazing!" said Brandon afterwards. "How do your feet move that fast? It's like watching a drum solo, except that the drumsticks are giant and wearing black pants."

They headed back to where they had camped. Along the way, Brandon grabbed Seth's arm.

"You're not going to believe what I just saw."

Seth smirked. "A girl you think looks hot? Gee, that was hard to predict."

"Mallory Lyons!" Brandon indicated a girl halfway across the ballroom.

Sure enough, the pretty cheerleader in street clothes walked beside another girl in a bright orange solo costume. "She's with Shelby. I guess that makes sense. They're both cheerleaders, so she's here watching her friend."

"I guess," said Brandon. "I just didn't expect to know any of the girls here. I like the idea of being a man of mystery."

After his second dance, Seth checked the results area and found he had placed first in his reel. He went to the awards table and picked up his gold medal. Brandon had remained at the camp area, keeping an eye on a girl a couple of blankets away who looked "promising".

As Seth turned back toward the ballroom, he almost ran into Mallory.

"Sorry," he said, flustered.

"Hi," said Mallory. "You're on the football team at Paavo, aren't you?"

Seth nodded warily. This was the way his first conversation with Shelby had started, and that had not turned out well.

"So you dance, too?" continued Mallory.

Seth felt his face redden. Was she going to call him "Twinkletoes" and make a joke about his dancing the way her boyfriend had?

"That's cool," said Mallory, flashing a perfect-teeth smile. "Shelby is getting ready for her next dance and I was just going to get a slice of pizza. Do you want to get some, too?"

In a few minutes, he found himself sitting at a table in the concessions area, eating pizza and talking about classes at Paavo High School. Eventually the conversation turned to Homecoming.

"Do you have a date yet?" asked Mallory.

Seth shook his head. "I still haven't met a lot of people since moving here. I guess you're going with Jason."

Mallory finished a sip of her soft drink and shrugged. "He hasn't asked me yet. And sometimes he can be kind of annoying, you know?"

Seth nodded as if he understood, although he was not at all certain that this was the case. Jason had annoyed him by making fun of his dancing. If Mallory found him annoying, he was certain it must be for far different reasons.

And what was going on here? Was Mallory trying to tell him something? Was she saying, "Hey! I'm available! Ask me to the dance! Could I make it any clearer, you moron?"

And because he was unsure, he said nothing. Except to excuse himself to get ready for his next dance.

"Hey, maybe we could hang out some time," suggested Mallory as he stood.

"Hang out?"

"Maybe you could come over and help me with chemistry," she explained. "You're in my second period class, right? I'm so lost right now that I know I'm going to fail the next test."

"Sure, I could help you," said Seth. "I'm doing pretty well."

Then he waved a pathetic goodbye and returned to the ballroom. He found Brandon still staring at the girl three blankets over.

"Subject has been sighted," he reported, cupping his hands around his eyes like binoculars. "We are locked and loaded and ready to fire!"

"What does that mean?" asked Seth.

"It means," said Brandon desperately, "that I have no idea what I'm going to do! I can't just walk up and start talking to a complete stranger!"

"I thought you said even a cadaver could get a date at a feis," said Seth.

"That's right," said Brandon. "But I meant a smooth-talking cadaver who is naturally charming around girls."

"Oh," said Seth, straightening his tie and vest, "*that* kind of cadaver." Then he remembered his medal and showed it to Brandon.

"Awesome!" said his friend. "It took you long enough to get back here. I'm glad it was worth the wait."

Seth then told his friend about the meeting with Mallory.

Brandon's jaw dropped. "It sounds like she was hitting on you! You, my man, are *that* kind of cadaver!"

"Thanks, I think," said Seth, and he headed off to stage three. On the way, though, he thought of Shelby and his heart sank. It was possible that he could end up as some kind of cadaver—if news of his lunch with Mallory ever made it back to Jason Troy.

Eleven

His feet hit the floor with the force of hammers. Dozens of hammers, tapping out a complex cacophony. Toes pointed and turned out, kicks high. Part gymnast, part figure skater, part Olympic sprinter: This was how Seth felt when he danced.

At the end of practice, Annie stopped near him as he changed out of his dance shoes.

"two firsts on Saturday. Impressive. Looks like you haven't lost much in the past two years."

Seth struggled to hide the smile. "But I still didn't get a first in my treble jig. That's the one I need."

"Be patient," said Annie. "You've had a long layoff. You should be proud of what you accomplished."

As Annie moved on to talk to other dancers, Seth spotted Shelby rummaging in her duffle bag a short distance away. If she knew that he had shared pizza with Mallory, she gave no indication. This made him feel better.

Friday's game was at Pilot Stadium against Scuppernong Springs. Again, the Pilots won easily — by four touchdowns.

"Now that's Pilot football!" roared Coach Wisk after the game. And then he actually smiled.

Another curious thing happened after the game, and Seth brought it to Brandon's attention as they sat in the Hangar waiting for nourishment.

"Do you see Jason with his buddies?" whispered Seth, pointing to a booth across the restaurant.

Brandon nodded. "So?"

"How come he's spending Friday night after the game with a bunch of guys rather than with Mallory?"

Brandon played with the salt shaker. "What's the big deal? I'm spending Friday evening with you!"

"But," continued Seth, "if you were dating a super-hot cheerleader, would you be here with me right now?"

"If I were dating a super-hot cheerleader, I'd be home asleep," said Brandon, "because the only way that's going to happen is in my dreams!" Then he added, "You're right. Unless he suffered brain damage in the game, Jason should be with her. Maybe they aren't a couple anymore!"

Their burgers and drinks arrived, courtesy of Brandon's sister.

"Don't throw it all over the wall this time," said Kimmy as she set the cups and plastic baskets in front of them.

Seth wanted to say something clever that would put Kimmy in her place. Nothing came to mind. As a result, he considered the wisdom of simply being earnest. *You know it was an accident*, he would say. Kimmy would not have a response for that. Or instead of honesty, perhaps he would . . .

Too late. Kimmy had already turned and flounced back behind the stainless steel service counter.

"It's only three weeks until Homecoming," blurted Brandon, snapping Seth back into the moment. "And I still don't know who to ask."

"I'm surprised you didn't find someone who was interested in you at the feis last Saturday," said Seth wryly.

"I did," countered Brandon. "But our school has a policy against bringing dates who are only ten years old."

Seth laughed with a mouthful of cola, spraying it all over the table. He looked up and saw Kimmy grabbing a wet rag and mop, shaking her head.

Seth had no more leads for a Homecoming date than did his friend—until the following Monday. In chemistry class, Mallory slid over to his work station during a lab.

"I think I'm understanding most of this, but I could still use some help writing it up," she told him. "Do you think you could come over tonight after football?"

Completely caught off guard, it took a moment before Seth understood the question. "Come over?"

"To my house," clarified Mallory.

When Brandon learned of this development at lunch, he almost forgot to eat his fourth and fifth chocolate chip cookies. "The hottest cheerleader in the entire cheerleading universe asked you over to her house to study? What did you say?"

When one is sixteen, male, and the hottest cheerleader in the cheerleading universe issues an invitation to her house to study, there is only one answer.

Seth walked to Mallory's house after practice. She lived only two blocks from Paavo High. His nervousness subsided a notch when Mrs. Lyons answered the door. She was tall, blonde like her daughter, and dressed in a way that made Seth think of a legal assistant from one of those crime investigation shows.

"So you're going to help Mallory with her chemistry," she said, ushering Seth inside. "That's very nice. You two can use the dining room table. You'll be able to spread out all of your papers."

An oak table rested at the approximate center of the room, although plenty of space remained around its perimeter. Paintings of garden scenes with children, slightly blurred, hung on the peach walls in antique, gold enameled frames. A large hutch upon which half a dozen plates were displayed rested against one wall and a broad, multi-paned window threw the fading light of the day across the oak floor. Seth set his backpack on a chair.

"I'll call Mallory."

Now the nervousness returned. When she arrived, would she recognize him for the ordinary, third-string, inexperienced-with-girls adolescent that he was and drive him from the house with cruel epithets?

Before he could fully imagine all the possible horrific scenarios, Mallory poked her head around the corner, smiled and uttered nothing more awful than a buoyant, "Hi!"

Mrs. Lyons brought soft drinks and the lab journals came out.

"This is where I get stuck," said Mallory, pointing to the section where she was supposed to analyze the lab data. Seth walked her through it, and as he did so, he could see the understanding come into her eyes.

"You make it seem so easy!" she said as they finished.

Seth felt good, confident, but also a bit disappointed. It was clear to him now that Mallory was simply interested in getting help with schoolwork. She had no interest in him as a Homecoming date. But then, when they finished, his confusion returned when she did not rush him out the door.

"Would you like something to eat?"

Seth checked his watch. "My mom will have supper ready in a little while."

Mallory made a pouty face. "How about a brownie? My mom's brownies are the best!"

Of course he could not refuse. Mallory disappeared out the door. *She's so . . . energetic,* thought Seth. *And she's the first girl I've really gotten to know who hasn't treated me like garbage.*

The nervousness returned, and Seth knew why. He was seriously considering asking Mallory to go to Homecoming with him.

Mallory reappeared with a plate full of brownies and a glass of milk. Seth had to admit that they were the best he had ever eaten.

As he ate, Mallory asked, "How was football practice?"

Seth decided to proceed carefully. He did not wish to mention Jason or anything that might steer the conversation toward him. It would be too awkward.

"I moved up to the fastest sprint group," he finally said.

Mallory beamed. "Some people say you have the fastest feet on the team."

Some people? Seth could hardly believe he had heard her correctly. *Some people were talking about me? About my feet?*

"They say," continued Mallory, "that it's the Irish dancing."

Seth felt his ears burn, but when he looked at Mallory's face, he saw no malice.

"That might have something to do with it, I guess."

Suddenly an idea seemed to come to her. "Can I see you do it?"

Seth almost choked on his brownie. "Dance?"

"Please? I went to one of those dance competitions with Shelby and it looked so awesome!"

On one hand, the thought of dancing in front of this super-cool, super-gorgeous creature seemed like the worst idea in the world. But when he was honest with himself, he realized that he would not be dancing for an unappreciative crowd of immature adolescents. He would be dancing only for her. It was possible that, based on what she had seen at the feis, Mallory really admired the speed and athleticism inherent in Irish dance. As he looked at the pleading sincerity in her eyes, Seth realized that for the first time since moving to Paavo, he had found someone who really understood—a kind of kindred spirit. If he had been just a little braver, he would have asked her to Homecoming right then and there. In fact, he probably would have leaned close and kissed her lightly on the lips, a kiss that both of them would remember all of their lives, an innocent kiss tasting slightly of excellent brownie and resonating with the nobility that blossoms when beauty and ordinariness intersect.

Instead, he stood.

"There's no music, so it won't be that good," he said lamely.

"That's okay." Her sincerity completely relaxed him, and he dropped his hands to his sides, standing in the wide space between the table and window. He imagined the hornpipe music in his head and moved as well as he could in the small space. It seemed to be good enough, for when he finished, Mallory clapped and laughed lightly and told him it was wonderful.

Breathing heavily, he now found himself at a loss for words. Then he remembered the time. "I guess I'd better go."

She thanked him for the help, walked him to the door.

Ask her now! He imagined Brandon's voice in his ear. *She thinks you're the god of chemistry and the lord of Irish dance! You can't lose! Ask her now!*

But then he found himself out on the sidewalk, heading home.

He would ask her tomorrow, he decided. In chemistry. Or after school, right before football practice. He began to jog down the sidewalk, unable to keep the smile from his face.

He was going to Homecoming with the best-looking girl at Paavo High School.

Twelve

"Wow!" That was all Brandon could say for several moments after Seth narrated the chain of events at Mallory's house. "You really know that a girl likes a guy when she asks him to Irish dance!"

Seth could hardly believe his good fortune. He had never really thought of himself as a guy capable of attracting a Hottest Cheerleader in the Cheerleading Universe kind of girl. He suspected he was a "nice looking young man" if his mother's opinion could be trusted. There had also been a very pretty girl back in St. Augustine. And there was Brandon's assessment: "Neither of us is overly hideous."

Yet, his Homecoming date was way beyond "nice looking". Mallory Lyons was teen-model amazing.

He hoped there would be no fallout associated with dating Mallory. Maybe everyone would wave, smile, give a thumb's up sign when they saw him—in his Pilots football jersey—walking beside her in the hallways at school. On the other hand, he might have to deal with jealous teammates, resentful that the new kid was taking Mallory to Homecoming. And how would Jason react? Was he *over* Mallory, or would Seth have to deal with that?

Seth had hoped for another chemistry lab, which allowed students to be out of their seats and moving around. Then he could have wandered to Mallory's work station and coolly tossed out the notion that the two of them might go to Homecoming. He imagined her wide, ready smile, just like last night, and her bubbly agreement. Then the God of Chemistry and Lord of Irish Dance would saunter back to his own station while the awed whispers swept the room.

Unfortunately, it was "notes day" in chemistry, which meant that they would be sitting quietly in their desks as Mrs. Archer explained Raoult's law on the board.

I'll ask her after class, Seth told himself.

Unfortunately, Mallory disappeared out the door quickly after class, and Seth had to console himself with the idea of asking her at lunch or after school.

However, getting to lunch would not be easy. In his third period American literature class, Seth knew that Mr. Burrows would be showing a film. It had been on the syllabus for a week, and Mr. Burrows was very excited about it. Something about life in colonial America: *The Pilgrims and the Wampanoags*.

Under normal circumstances, Seth suspected that he would enjoy the movie event about as much as forty-five minutes of dental work. Today, his mind unable to focus on anything other than Mallory Lyons and Homecoming, he was pretty sure he would not remember a single second of the film.

Mr. Burrows offered a few opening remarks calculated to pump up his teenaged audience and to link the subject matter of the film to the essays, journal entries and stories that they were reading. Then he dimmed the lights and clicked the appropriate button on his remote. The monitor at the front of the classroom flickered to life and the image of a teenage boy appeared. The boy was dancing.

He was dancing the hornpipe.

And he was doing it in Mallory Lyons' dining room.

A few people snickered as they recognized Seth on the screen. Mr. Burrows heard the laughter and glanced up from his paperwork. "That's not the video about Plymouth Colony." Then he sought out Seth, who tried unsuccessfully to sink beneath his desk. "That looks like you, Mr. Kerrighan." His eyes darted around the room. "Is this supposed to be a joke?"

Most of the students had quieted again, except for Jason Troy, Danny Sidowski and a blond boy sitting near them, who continued to snicker as if someone had just crippled a puppy.

Mr. Burrows frowned in their direction. "That will do, Mr. Troy."

Their laughing stopped now, but their heads turned slightly so that they caught Seth's eye. As Mr. Burrows removed the maverick CD and found the correct one resting in his chalk tray, Jason and his pals flashed wide, rotten smiles.

Seth wished he could get up and leave. Maybe go to the nurse's room. Or just go home. He actually felt nauseous—and sickeningly hot. Most of all, he felt mortally embarrassed and hurt to the edges of his soul.

It was all so clear to him now.

Mallory had never been interested in him. Jason had simply used her. Maybe Jason had been at Mallory's house the previous night, filming him from the next room. Or maybe the camera had been hidden in the hutch and Mallory had turned it on when she had gone to get the plate of brownies.

His stomach churned. He had really liked those brownies. And Mallory. He wanted to scream, to throw his books.

To cry.

But all he could do was sit silently and watch frightened pilgrims attempt to build a fortress against the untold horrors of a savage, new world.

Thirteen

He talked to no one, kept his eyes to the floor, walked swiftly. Seth's only desire was to avoid having to say anything to anyone for the remainder of the school day. His anger had grown since the embarrassing video, and so had the hurt. Being a member of the Paavo football team was supposed to make you popular. It was supposed to guarantee that girls would like you.

The exact opposite had occurred.

In fact, he hardly felt like he was a member of the football team at all. In a way, that hurt more than being tricked by Mallory. Seth loved football. He knew his father had loved it, too. But things had been different in St. Augustine.

That's why he was skipping lunch, heading to Coach Blair's office.

He strode resolutely down the hallway, across the empty gymnasium, and into another short hallway that contained the offices for the coaching staff. Coach Blair's door stood open and Seth marched right in.

"Coach, I'm—"

But it was Coach Wisk who sat behind the desk.

"Well, you look like you're on a mission, son."

Seth glanced around the room. "I was looking for Coach Blair."

Coach Wisk flexed his facial muscles impatiently. "He's not here right now. Maybe I can help, if it's that important. Looks like you got something on your mind."

Seth considered this turn of events. He had wanted to talk to Coach Blair, but in the long run, Blair or Wisk, it really didn't matter. He tried to gather his energy again, mostly succeeded.

"I'm quitting the team, sir."

Coach Wisk raised an eyebrow. "Quitting? Why would you quit the Pilots, son?"

He struggled to put his feelings into words— not because he had trouble finding the words, but because of the pain that he knew would come from speaking them out loud. "Everybody hates me, sir. They do cruel things to me. I don't feel like I belong."

The coach's face betrayed little emotion. "What sort of things have they done to you?"

Why couldn't Coach Wisk just shake his hand and send him on his way? Why was he asking so many questions, making it so difficult?

"They make fun of me. Put signs on my locker. Call me names."

Coach Wisk squinted at him, his wide, creased face reminding Seth of a possum with a crewcut. "Why would they make fun of you?"

Seth did not want to have this discussion, but he felt compelled to answer Coach Wisk's question.

"I'm an Irish dancer. They make fun of my dancing."

Coach Wisk nodded slowly, silently, and after a long moment, leaned forward onto the desk. "Maybe you need to start acting like a man, son."

"Sir?"

"They're making fun of you? Boo-hoo. What are you going to do, run away every time someone criticizes one of your little zits or the color of your socks?"

Seth always felt intimidated by Coach Wisk, but he now began to feel angry, too. "This is a little different than socks."

Coach Wisk shrugged. "If it bothers you so much, maybe you should quit the dancing. If you devoted that time to something really worthwhile, like football, then maybe you'd start playing like a champion. Do you think you'll ever be the quarterback of this football team as long as you're dancing? The dancing quarterback! That's not going to earn their respect!"

Seth felt as if someone had punched him in the gut, taking away his wind. He wanted to reach across the desk and grab Coach Wisk by the collar and scream in his face—although Coach Wisk probably would have broken him in half with no more effort than if he were snapping a pencil.

Luckily, Coach Blair walked in and broke the tension. He smiled at Seth. "Decide to skip lunch? Talk strategy?"

Coach Wisk indicated Seth with a thumb. "Kerrighan here wants to go pansy on us."

Coach Blair's forehead wrinkled. "Go pansy?"

"He wants to quit the team," explained Wisk as if he were talking about a moldy sandwich he had found in the fridge. "His teammates aren't sensitive enough to his feelings."

Blair now looked at Seth, then back towards Wisk. "Why don't you give me and Seth a minute. See if we can sort this out."

Reluctantly, Wisk rose from the chair and disappeared out the doorway. Coach Blair closed the door and sat in his vacated seat, inviting Seth into a chair across the desk. He looked at Seth for a moment with stern yet sympathetic eyes.

"So you really want to quit?"

Seth's eyes sought the floor, but then he brought them up to meet Coach Blair's and repeated what he had told Wisk. He added a description of the "Twinkletoes" episode in the locker room, the end of which Blair had witnessed. Coach Blair listened quietly and sat considering the matter after Seth had finished.

"I'd heard you were taking dance lessons," Blair said finally.

"I compete, sir."

Coach Blair appeared surprised. "In Irish dance? How does it work? Is it like in those TV shows where you have a partner?

Seth shook his head. "You dance without a partner, but there's another dancer on stage at the same time. A judge looks at footwork, speed, timing, positioning, height of your jumps . . . everything! I've traveled all over the Midwest, though not this year. I didn't dance the last couple years when we lived in St. Augustine. There's thousands of dancers at some competitions."

Coach Blair's eyes widened.

"I don't dance against all of them," Seth added hastily. "Only the ones in my age group."

Coach Blair leaned back. "Why'd you come back?"

"Come back?"

"To dancing," clarified Coach Blair. "You said you didn't dance when you lived in St. Aug."

"I thought it would help me for football, give me faster feet."

"For football?" Coach Blair paused. "Well, what do you think? Did the dancing help?"

Seth nodded. "I think so."

Blair leaned forward, folded his arms onto the blotter atop his desk. "I noticed you moved up to the first sprint group."

"Yes sir."

His answer hung in the air for a long moment.

"Let me ask you something," said Coach Blair. "And keep in mind, I'm not asking you to give me names or anything like that. How many guys on the team do you think put those signs up in the locker room?"

Seth considered it. "One or two, I guess."

"How many laughed?" asked Blair.

The incident stood out as clear as a moment ago in his memory. "Probably half the team."

The corner of Blair's mouth curled into a smile. "Only half?" His next question caught Seth off-guard. "Would you have laughed?"

"Me?"

"Yeah. That muscle cream you guys use, the stuff that burns like fire, if someone had put that ointment in a teammate's jockstrap, would you have laughed?"

Seth had actually seen this happen to someone at St. Augustine. "Yeah, I guess."

"Of course you would," continued Blair. "That doesn't make it right. But high school kids are human and they're adolescents and they're sometimes going to laugh at foolish, even cruel behavior. Now, how many of them kept laughing? You know, after everyone made noise, did anyone keep after you? Taunting? Saying things on your way out of the locker room or the next day, maybe?"

"Maybe one or two," Seth admitted.

"And is this the same one or two that have continued to give you a rough time?"

Seth nodded.

Blair let it sink in. "Son, you don't want to quit. It's not the whole team. It's a few guys who have some growing up to do and who don't understand that being a member of a team means you support the other guys, you don't tear them down."

It was true, Seth thought. He was friends with Brandon and a few other guys on the team. Most of the rest were indifferent to him. Only Jason, Danny and a couple of their pals had ever wanted to hurt him. That was maybe four out of about eighty varsity players.

"Thanks, Coach." Seth stood to leave.

"One more thing," said Coach Blair. "Football means a lot to you, doesn't it?"

Seth nodded.

"Don't ever let anybody make you give up something you love," said Blair. "Or make you feel embarrassed about it."

"Yes sir," said Seth.

"Not football," added Coach Blair, "and not dance."

Fourteen

Seth completed four of five passes against the first-string defense in practice on Wednesday. Coach Wisk mercilessly berated the defensive backs each time, and—at one point—seemed dangerously close to giving Seth a compliment.

At dance practice, Seth told Annie about his conversation with Coach Blair.

"His advice sounded a lot like what you told me," said Seth. "That it was only a few people."

Annie smiled. "Great minds think alike."

The Friday game was a solid 21-7 win for Paavo over a pretty good McMiller High team. Jason completed seven of eleven passes and rushed for fifty yards. Most importantly, the win gave Paavo a 4-1 record. With four regular-season games remaining, they needed only one more win to guarantee a spot in the state playoffs, where they would have a shot at revenge against Drumlin.

After the game, Brandon suggested a change from their usual routine. "It's Eddie Cooper's birthday! They're throwing a birthday party for him at Hanson's!"

"Should we stop and get a card?" asked Seth as they piled into Brandon's car.

Brandon gave him the idiot look. "We'll just grab a bag of chips on the way!"

Elliot Hanson was a tight end, and Brandon seemed to know the way to his house, located about four miles outside of Paavo. When they turned in at the driveway, Seth saw only two cars parked near the house. He remarked in surprise that there did not seem to be many people at the birthday party.

"Hanson's parents built that house six years ago," explained Brandon as he cruised past the nice-looking brick home and continued down the long, gravel drive. "All of this land is theirs. About a hundred acres, I guess. Hanson's father and grandfather both farmed it. Anyway, before they built the new brick house, they lived in this old farmhouse at the end of a mile-long driveway. Now it just sits back there by itself, surrounded by trees and farmland—except when Hanson has a party! It's the perfect place because nobody will bother us!"

After another minute, Brandon's headlights revealed the old farmhouse, a dark, looming two-story building. At least twenty cars were parked along the driveway and in the overgrown yard. Brandon found a spot and the two boys headed toward the house. Seth noticed that he could see his breath and was glad he had worn his letter jacket.

Music issued vaguely from somewhere behind the house. As the two boys stepped inside, Seth noticed several camping lanterns that provided enough light to get them to the kitchen. Apparently the Hansons had cut off the power to their old house when they had moved to the new one. Another camping lantern rested at the center of an old table in the kitchen, and Brandon tossed their bag of chips beside it with a dozen others. Then they pushed open the back door and descended several wooden steps into the eye of the party storm.

A bonfire blazed in the backyard about thirty feet from the house. Off to the right sat a metal tub filled with ice and a smorgasbord of wines and liquors. A second tub contained a quarter barrel.

"Do Hanson's parents know about this?" asked Seth anxiously.

"They've got cows to milk in the morning," said Brandon dismissively. "They were probably in bed and asleep fifteen minutes after the end of the football game."

Still Seth felt uncomfortable. "Just about the whole team is here."

"Eddie Cooper's a popular guy," noted Brandon.

"But," implored Seth, "what if the party gets busted? We could get suspended from the team for being at a beer party!"

"Relax," said Brandon. "No one's going to get busted. Hanson's driveway is so long that we could set off an atomic bomb out here and the cops in Paavo would never know it."

Brandon led them to a boy in a Hawaiian shirt slouched in a lawn chair near the fire. "Happy birthday, Coop!"

Cooper attempted to give Brandon a high-five, but missed and nearly tumbled out of the chair.

Next, Brandon visited the quarter-barrel, filling a plastic cup with beer. He picked up a second cup, but Seth waved him off.

"What are you, some kind of saint?" asked Brandon.

Seth shoved his hands into his jacket pockets and shivered now that they were some distance from the fire. "Someone once told me that if you stay away from drugs and alcohol and play by the rules, you'll go farther."

Brandon sneered. "Who said that?"

"My dad," said Seth. "Maybe I'll see if I can find a cola."

War whoops sounded from the direction of the fire, and Seth turned to see that a couple of football players had removed their shirts and were performing a bare-chested dance in the flickering light. Now, as his attention was drawn to the far side of the blaze, Seth noticed there were girls at the party. Not many, but he identified three cheerleaders and a couple others who he thought were probably seniors. One of the girls was wrapping Cooper in toilet paper as he sat there in his lawn chair, staring into the flames.

"Hey Twink!"

The voice came from the direction of the back steps, and Seth turned to see Jason, his arm draped across Mallory's shoulders.

"Let's see a dance, Twink!" called Jason. "Let's see those lightning feet!"

Mallory giggled. So did Danny Sidowski and a kid standing next to him. But as Seth looked around, he realized that Coach Blair and Annie had been right. No one else seemed to care.

"I'll pass," said Seth.

"I want to see how fast you are!" said Jason. Seth could tell he had been drinking, although he was nowhere near as far along as the guest of honor.

"I guess you'll have to wait until practice to see me," said Seth, changing direction to head to the far side of the fire.

"We certainly won't see it in a game!" cried Danny, and then he and his buddy burst into laughter. A couple of cheerleaders also laughed, but it seemed to Seth that they were laughing mostly because Danny and his pal thought the statement had been so over-the-top funny.

"I want to see how fast you are!" said Danny. "Jason will race you right now, won't you Jace?"

Now everyone was looking at Seth. He turned to Brandon. "Let's get out of here."

"Race him, Seth," whispered Brandon.

Seth's face contorted in disbelief. "Are you nuts?"

Brandon pulled his ear close. "If you beat him, he and Danny will have to respect you."

"Brandon, he was all-conference!" Seth reminded him. "He's the fastest guy on the team! He wins every sprint in practice!"

"And you've been moving up every week," argued Brandon. "You just made it into the first sprint group. You don't know yet how fast you are."

"Brandon!"

"You haven't been tested!"

Danny interrupted. "Let's go, dance boy! Let's see what you got! Or are you too good for us? Is that why you parade around in that red and black letter jacket instead of a Pilots jacket?"

"It's too dark," said Seth desperately. "We'd trip and break our necks."

"We can turn a couple of car headlights down the driveway and you can run there," suggested a tall, red-haired kid.

A few people clapped at the novelty of the idea, and in another moment, Seth felt himself swept along toward the front of the house. He was pushed onto the driveway where he found Jason in his Paavo football jersey, his green and white Paavo letter jacket off. Two cars pulled up behind them and the headlights burst on, throwing beams a hundred yards down the straight dirt-and-gravel surface.

Seth removed his St. Augustine jacket and stood beside Jason. *I guess we're really doing this.* Brandon thought he could beat Jason. But Seth knew that was crazy. Still, even losing might have its advantages. When Jason had shown everyone he was the better man, Seth hoped he and Danny would finally be satisfied and just leave him alone.

The red-haired kid ran the hundred yards to where the lights played out in order to judge the finish. Everyone else hopped on top of the cars parked along the road to get a better vantage point.

I hadn't realized that there were so many people!

"I'll say ready, set and then honk my horn!" called Danny from behind.

"Hey," said Jason, turning his head toward Seth. "Prepare to be toasted, Twink!"

Everyone hooted and called out, mostly in support of Jason.

I should have gone to the Hangar as usual. Watching Kimmy clean up my messes is more fun than this. Then he thought, *Cleaning up my own mess would be more fun than this.*

"All right!" called Danny. "On your marks!"

The cries got louder.

"Get set!"

Seth's heart pounded as he leaned into the ready position.

Danny's horn blared and Seth exploded down the driveway, kicking up dirt and stones. Air burst from his lungs in fierce clouds and he felt himself rise onto his toes. The shouts and cheers of the teens perched atop cars dissolved into a kind of distant white noise as he sped down the road, replaced by what seemed to be the distant pulse of hornpipe music. As he passed red-hair, the sound of the real world poured back in on him and he heard Jason's footfall—a half-second behind. When Seth slowed and turned, he saw the star quarterback bent over, panting, hands on his knees.

Now the watchers leaped off of cars and pickup trucks, bounding toward the runners. Seth heard the mangle of voices:

"Did you see that?"

"I didn't think anyone was faster than Jason!"

"Who is he, anyway? Does he go to Paavo? His jacket was red and black."

Then the watchers slowed, keeping a wary-eyed distance as Jason straightened himself and faced Seth. He looked Seth over for a moment as if seeing him clearly for the first time. Then he seemed to consider the approaching crowd behind him, to remember that he was Jason Lyons and that he was also the captain of the Pilots football team.

"Nice job, Kerrighan," said Jason, between panting breaths. "I'd race you again right now, but I think I'd puke! Be ready in practice on Monday!" Then he extended his right hand, and Seth, although startled, shook it.

This seemed to break the spell over the watchers, who began to chatter loudly again. Jason had taken it like a man, they seemed to agree. That's why he was the leader of the Pilots. But this new kid was pretty fast. Where did he come from?

"The way everybody acts, you'd think we raced to a tie," said Seth as Brandon sprinted up and pounded his palm good-naturedly on his friend's back.

"Jason's the golden boy," said Brandon. "The first pitcher to strike out Babe Ruth didn't exactly get carried off the field and into baseball history."

"Babe Ruth struck out a lot," said Seth. But he knew his friend was right. One race wasn't going to change everything.

On the other hand, it was a start. Jason had shaken his hand. And he had seen a dawning respect in the eyes of many of the watchers.

Many—but not all.

Seth turned to the sound of tires spinning on gravel and a yellow pickup truck roared down the road, causing several teens to leap out of the way. "Yee-haw!" yelled the driver.

"It's Sidowski," growled Brandon. "He's so messed up, he's got no more business driving than Coop does."

Danny braked hard, sending a dusty cloud into the headlights that continued to blaze. Then he turned so he was sideways on the road and called out the driver's window.

"You proved you're a Pilot tonight, Twink!" yelled Danny, a big, stupid smile plastered across his face. "So it's about time you looked like a Pilot rather than like you're from some two-dollar, hick school!"

At first, Seth did not get Danny's meaning. Then he saw his red and black St. Augustine letter jacket, hanging like a flag from a pole or tree branch jammed vertically into a slot in the wall of the pickup's bed.

"Hey!"

He took a quick step toward the pickup, but Danny gunned the engine and he stopped. Seth felt his heart pound. A moment later his anger surged as he realized that the jacket had been mutilated. The black "A" on the front had been removed—his varsity letter, the one his father had been so proud of. Threads still dangled from where it had been torn off. As if this weren't enough, it looked like a crude "P" had been drawn in its place.

"Where's my letter?" asked Seth, trying hard to control his voice. He took another step toward the truck, but Danny cranked the wheel and gave it a little gas, keeping it just out of Seth's reach.

"It's on your jacket!" yelled Danny. "P for Pilots!"

Seth could not keep from shouting. "Where is it?" Another lunge, more gas, and Danny idled the truck just ahead.

In answer, Danny looked toward the bonfire. "Burn, baby, burn!"

No! Seth wanted to pull Danny from the truck and smash his face. Never had he felt such hatred.

He burst ahead again, but all Danny had to do was give the truck a bit more gas to send it forward another fifty feet where he stopped again and grinned back at his pursuer.

Then a voice to his right surprised Seth. "All right, Danny, give him the jacket."

It was Jason who spoke, but Danny's eyes remained dark, fixed on Seth. After another moment, Danny flashed a shiny smile and yelled, "If he's so fast, he can come get it himself!"

Jason jogged a couple steps toward the truck and leaped onto the tailgate. Then he reached up to lift the jacket off the rough stick from which it dangled. However, Danny's attention was still focused on Seth, and as he took another step forward, Danny stomped on the gas pedal once again, sending the truck lurching forward. The sudden movement caught Jason completely off guard, sending him tumbling backward, first against the side wall of the truck's bed and then out the tailgate.

The sickening sound Jason made when he hit the ground and the wrenching cry that burst from him convinced Seth that he was hurt badly.

He prayed that he was wrong.

Fifteen

A pall hung over Homecoming week, an almost palpable gloom that virtually every student could feel. Jason Troy had a broken throwing arm and a separated shoulder.

The team meeting room suffered a broken chair, courtesy of Coach Wisk's foot. "Out for the season!" roared the coach. "All because of a lot of foolishness!"

Although the exact details of the incident remained hazy, the general population had heard rumors of a party and some ensuing rowdiness. No individuals had been named, but one could tell who had attended the forbidden event by the way eyes were averted.

Coach Wisk's tirade lasted twenty minutes. Then Coach Blair spoke slowly, carefully, first emphasizing his disappointment. "Drinking and partying doesn't show much of a commitment to being champions," he said. "I would have expected more from Paavo football players."

The quiet words hurt far worse that Coach Wisk's verbal grenades. Every head hung in shame.

Then Blair reminded them that the world would not stop spinning simply because some individuals had made foolish decisions. "Danny's probably the best back-up quarterback in the league. He could probably start for most of the teams. We will miss Jason's expertise and leadership, but we have many fine players on this team, and now is their opportunity to step up and accept the challenge."

By the time they finally took the practice field on Monday, everyone felt relieved and confident — although by no means did they feel forgiven.

Danny looked great in practice, throwing the ball accurately, calling effective plays. "It's almost like Jason is still out there behind center," admitted Brandon.

Seth did not know how to feel. His anger toward Danny had not abated. His varsity letter was ashes. And he blamed Danny for Jason's injury — although he felt partly to blame himself.

"It's not like you did anything wrong," Brandon pointed out.

Seth shrugged. "I know. But it was my jacket."

"But look at it this way," said Brandon. "You're one step closer to being the starting quarterback!"

Seth frowned. "Oh, yeah. It's a great feeling knowing that you're second-string because some guy fell off a truck!"

Being second-string bothered Seth for another reason, which he did not share with any of his friends. Annie Delaney, however, noticed something in his demeanor at dance practice.

"You seem . . . distracted," she told Seth. "It's like you're just going through the motions today. Usually your steps are so full of life!"

He told her about Jason's accident. "Now I've started thinking about what would happen if Danny got hurt."

Annie looked surprised. "You'd be out there on the field, quarterbacking the Pilots. Isn't that what you wanted?"

"I thought I did," said Seth. "But now it scares me."

"You know," said Annie, "pretty soon you're going to be a Preliminary Champion dancer. You'll be competing on one of the main stages at every feis. And instead of one judge, there will be three judges watching every move you make. Does that make you nervous?"

Seth shrugged. "Sure. But it's just three judges. When you take the football field for the Pilots, there could be a couple thousand people watching you!"

"But didn't you quarterback your team at St. Augustine last year?" asked Annie.

"The crowds were a lot smaller," noted Seth.

"But I'll bet you were still nervous for your first game."

Now Seth smiled. "I was. I must have used the bathroom seven times in the last half hour before the game. My dad kept hurrying me up, trying to get me out onto the field."

Annie smiled, too. "What happened when the game started?"

Seth thought about it. "After the first play, I didn't even think about the crowd anymore. It's like they weren't even there. We were just playing football. It's like in Irish dance. When I'm waiting, I'm nervous. Once the dance starts, I don't think about it anymore."

"I'll bet it'll be that way if you get into the game for Paavo, too," said Annie. "Whether there are two hundred or two thousand in the stands, you'll be focused on the game. Think about it, Seth. You started Irish dancing when you were twelve. It taught you to get up in front of people and to perform fearlessly. If you get into the game, you're going to do great!"

Seth met Annie's eyes. "Can I ask you a favor?"

"What?"

"Can you stand next to me on the sidelines, and if coach calls my number, can you give me that pep talk right before I go into the game?"

Sixteen

The week was filled with the usual Homecoming excitement. Decorations had begun appearing in the hallways and common areas on Monday. Now, on Thursday, every athlete's locker sported some sort of decoration, and posters advertised special events, including Saturday's dance.

Brandon and Seth still had no dates, but many students were going as "singles", and so both had purchased tickets.

"Lots of girls are going as singles, too," Brandon told him at lunch on Thursday. "It's going to be great!"

Seth did not feel the greatness of the impending weekend. A sense of doom hung in the air, a doom that was somehow connected to him. Because of his jacket, the best quarterback in the conference was injured. And if something happened to the number two quarterback, the fate of the game would rest in Seth's hands. Annie was wrong. He had never felt like this going into an Irish dancing competition.

All was lost.

School dismissed an hour early on Friday so that students could attend a pep assembly in the gymnasium. Seth and Brandon participated in the group cheers and clapped enthusiastically for the Homecoming court—Jason and Mallory were voted king and queen, of course—but inside, Seth wished he were anywhere else. As he watched the senior class adviser place the king's crown on Jason's head, saw Jason smiling and waving his one good arm at the crowd, he felt almost physically ill.

"I'll see you later," he said to Brandon.

"Where you going? You're going to miss the parade!"

"Feeling a little crummy," he told his friend. "Gonna try and get some rest before the game."

He exited the gymnasium through a fire door and found himself at the back of the school where the Homecoming floats had been constructed. The area appeared mostly deserted except for a single faculty member standing watch about a hundred yards away, and a couple of students who had opted to miss the pep assembly in order to make last minute adjustments to their tissue-covered creations. A dozen floats awaited the start of the parade. They would loop through Paavo's downtown and then back to the high school, accompanied by the marching band, convertibles carrying the

Homecoming court members, two or three fire engines and a few floats provided by local businesses. About two hours after that, the big game against Rosemary would kick off. Just the thought of it made his stomach churn again.

It couldn't be just any team. No, the most important game of the year would be against their biggest rival. His stomach gurgled and it occurred to Seth that he might just toss his lunch onto the back wall of the high school.

Focus, he told himself, and almost without a thought, his feet began to move. Like manic hammers they tapped out the steps of his hornpipe, tracing the dance's powerful, intricate pattern.

And somehow, he felt better—more confident.

"I guess you're not as clumsy as I thought," said a voice from one of the floats. Seth turned sharply and saw Kimmy atop a float, adjusting the bandana on a stuffed figure that looked to be a pirate.

Seth felt embarrassed and looked away.

"How come you're not in there with the rest of the howling mob?" asked Kimmy.

He turned back toward her but avoided eye contact. "Guess I just needed to get away from it. Kind of nervous about the game." Then he added, "I should have guessed that pep rallies wouldn't be your thing."

"I have nothing against pep rallies," said Kimmy. "I'll start going to them as soon as they have one for the drama club." She pointed to the float on which she stood, and Seth now saw that it had been built by the dancers, singers and actors of that organization.

"Why pirates?" asked Seth, pointing.

Kimmy pointed to a papier-mâché pirate ship that appeared to be sinking into a blue-tissue sea. "The team we're playing tonight, Rosemary, their mascot is the Mariners. Mariners travel by boat. And since we're doing the musical Pirates of Penzance this year, we thought this would be clever." The stuffed pirate next to which Kimmy stood was being run through by a sword held by a second stuffed figure in a Pilots football uniform.

"Yeah, that's a great ship," said Seth, who then turned to leave. "I guess I'd better—"

"Hey!" interrupted Kimmy. "How'd you learn to dance like that? My brother said you were an Irish dancer, but I didn't know it looked like that. Pretty amazing."

Seth smiled. "Thanks." He turned again to go, but then looked back. "Your float's pretty amazing, too."

The team met after the parade in the cafeteria for a light supper and then the players relaxed in the locker room until it was time to don their uniforms and stare at the Bobby Farrell ball. As Seth pulled on his immaculately clean number eight jersey, he prayed that Danny would not get hurt.

"Feeling better?" asked Brandon, who slid onto the bench next to him. "Because now I'm nervous! I've been to the bathroom three times in the last twenty minutes!"

"Don't remind me!" said Seth, and both boys suddenly headed off to find to toilet again.

At ten minutes to seven, Coach Blair gathered the team for a few words of inspiration and then jogged them to the field where the lights already blazed and the crowd roared in anticipation. They spent the next half-hour drilling and stretching on half the field. The red-and-white Mariners did the same on their half. Just before seven-thirty, Jason in his sling and two other Pilots met the referees and the Mariner captains at center field for the coin toss. The Pilots won the toss and elected to kick. This meant that Rosemary would be kicking to Paavo to start the second half. As Jason jogged off the field, he waved his good arm to the crowd, which gave him a standing ovation. This got Seth's stomach going again.

Rosemary started with the ball on their own thirty-one yard line. However, they made it only to mid-field before their drive stalled and they punted it away. After the return, the officials spotted the football on the Paavo twenty-four yard line.

"All right, Danny!" yelled Coach Wisk, slapping the quarterback on his shoulder pads. "Let's show 'em how the Pilots treat their Homecoming guests!"

Don't get hurt! At this point, Seth decided that Danny could have burned down his entire house and he would still have cheered madly for his success.

Danny half-turned toward the bench to grab his helmet, and then jogged out to the huddle.

Brandon could not contain his excitement. "I'll bet Danny marches us right down the field!"

"I hope so," said Seth. But if he had been worried before, now Seth felt himself on the verge of a new level of anxiety. When Danny had turned to grab his helmet, Seth had caught a glimpse of his face. Perhaps it had been the lights. Perhaps he had not gotten a good look due to how quickly it all happened. Still, he could have sworn that Danny's eyes had seemed unfocused, almost as if he were trying to will himself someplace else.

Almost as if he were scared.

Seventeen

Halftime score: Rosemary Mariners 14, Paavo Pilots 6.

Seth swore that a vein in Coach Wisk's forehead was going to pop as he launched into his locker room tirade.

"Is this how you want to be remembered?" roared Wisk. "As the team that couldn't make a first down and lost their Homecoming game? Where's your pride? Where's your guts? Let's give Danny a little support!"

Even Brandon's eyes popped open in response to this statement. If anyone had played a sub-par game up to this point, it was Danny Sidowski. He had looked nothing like the infallible replacement that had dominated the practice field all week long. In the first half, he had completed only one of five passes, had rushed for three yards and had fumbled the snap once to give the ball back to Rosemary deep in Paavo territory.

"What's wrong with him?" whispered Brandon. "Even you could play better that what he's doing."

Seth scowled. "Gee, thanks."

"At least our defense is playing brilliantly," said Brandon. "We're still only down one touchdown. A score and a two-point conversion and we're tied!"

Coach Blair spoke without yelling during the halftime, but his message was clear: Stay focused and simply perform as if it were a weekday. "It doesn't matter whether you're running the plays in practice or in front of a thousand people in the stands—concentrate on the fundamentals. Some of you guys have been playing this game since you were eight or nine years old. You know how to handle big game situations without freezing. Now get back out there and be great!"

To Seth, it sounded very similar to the pep talk that Annie had given him.

Rosemary kicked off to Paavo to start the second half, and the Pilots returned the kick to their own forty-one.

"All right, that's our best field position of the night!" yelled Wisk. "Let's go, Danny. Let's ram it down their throats!"

Paavo lined up and Danny took the snap, dropping back for a pass. A couple of Paavo receivers broke free and Seth expected to see Danny loft a pass to one of them, but instead, Danny raised the ball and then brought it down as if he were not sure. All at once, a Mariner lineman broke through and sacked Danny for a four-yard loss.

"Come on, come on!" Seth heard himself muttering as Danny dropped back on second down. Again, two receivers popped open and Seth anticipated the pass. But again, Danny hesitated, and then he threw the ball too late, as if trying to force it to the memory of the once-open receiver. A Rosemary defender stepped in front, caught the ball against his chest, pulled it in and sprinted down the sideline untouched.

"Touchdown Mariners," said the announcer flatly. With the conversion, Rosemary trailed 21-6.

"This is bad," groaned Brandon.

As Mariner players slapped high-fives, the Paavo kick return team trudged onto the field. As Seth watched them go, he heard his name.

"Kerrighan!"

He turned to see Coach Blair pointing to him. "Warm up your arm! We're going to give you a try!" Blair rolled a football, which came to rest in front of Seth.

Brandon's eyes snapped wide. "You're going in!"

Other eyes widened, too. Coach Wisk's expression seemed to suggestion that a grave mistake had been made. And Danny's eyes first displayed shock, then anger. His lips curled and he stomped toward the end of the bench.

"Good luck, dance boy!" growled Danny as he passed, the words like muddy sleet. He gave the ball in front of Seth a frustrated kick—just as Seth reached for it. The kick caught Seth's right hand hard, and the ball squirted sideways. Seth grimaced and turned away, stepping behind the bench to cradle his injury. Only Brandon seemed to realize what had happened.

"Are you okay?" asked Brandon, following him. "Let's see?"

The middle finger on Seth's throwing hand already appeared swollen.

"It's probably a bruise," said Brandon. "Grab the ball and take a couple of throws."

Seth found he could hold onto the ball somewhat, but the pressure required to get off a decent throw made the pain shoot through his hand like electricity.

"I think the middle finger is broken," said Seth.

"This is a nightmare!" groaned Brandon. "Wisk is going to explode!"

"Kerrighan!"

Blair was calling him into the game. Seth turned, trotted to the sideline for his instructions.

As he walked onto the field, the crowd seemed to offer a different sort of buzz, as if waiting to see what would happen now. "Number eight, Seth Kerrighan, is now in at quarterback for the Pilots," said the announcer, although the voice seemed more incredulous than confident.

Seth did not feel particularly confident, either. His finger throbbed.

He called the play in the huddle, a simple dive that required him only to hand off the ball. As he brought the team to the line, the immensity of the crowd smacked him in the face.

You're not in St. Augustine anymore.

He barked the cadence and the center snapped him the ball. He groaned as it slapped against his swollen finger, and he lost it for a moment. Then he found the ball on the ground near his feet and dove onto it.

"Kerrighan recovers his own fumble!" blared the announcer. "Second down and eleven!"

Seth glanced at the sidelines where Blair stood impassively. Wisk, on the other hand, glared at him as if Seth were a trespasser.

On second down, Seth managed to complete the handoff, and Anderson gained three yards.

"Third down and eight!" reported the announcer.

All right. We're going in the right direction.

The fullback, Stumpner, brought in the third down play from Blair: a pass to one of the two wide receivers, who would cut toward the sidelines. A third receiver would head up the middle. Even with a good right hand, hitting the sideline pass was a tough assignment. He might be able to get the man over the middle, but he would have to be accurate and get some speed on the ball. With a broken middle finger, he doubted that was possible. On the other hand, he could not call a different play. The team was behind by two touchdowns. He had never played in a game for Paavo in his life. It would be suicide to try and override the coach's wishes.

As they broke huddle, the crowd rose to its feet. The Paavo fans were hungry for something good to finally happen. They disliked seeing their team being manhandled at its own Homecoming game by its biggest rival. The Rosemary fans smelled blood in the water. They were up by two touchdowns and Paavo was down to its third-string quarterback.

Seth had felt so confident after talking to Annie. But that had been before he had broken his finger, and before he had stood on the turf in front of two thousand screaming fanatics. What was it she had said about Irish dance?

It taught you to get up in front of people and to perform fearlessly.

Had it really? He closed his eyes, imagined standing on stage at a feis. The judge sat at a table thirty feet in front of him, eyes locked with his. The music began and his feet moved like black lightning, his arms straight at his sides.

Seth's eyes popped open. *Irish dancers don't use their arms.* He might not be able to pass, but his feet were fine. And he had beaten Jason Troy in a race.

He called the team to the line, took the snap, dropped back. Two receivers were covered. The wide man on the right was open, but Seth knew he would never be able to make the throw, so he brought the ball down and took off around the right side, cutting in and scooting past the diving linebacker for a nine-yard gain.

"First down, Paavo!" called the announcer, and this time there really was some enthusiasm in his voice.

Seth popped off the ground and headed back to the huddle, where his teammates knocked helmets and patted him on the shoulder pads. Then he drove the team down the field, using his running backs to pick up a short chunk of yardage here and there, and then scrambling in passing situations. On second down from the twelve yard line, Blair called a draw to Anderson, and it worked to perfection.

"Touchdown Paavo!"

The crowd erupted as the scoreboard flashed 21-13.

Suddenly, Paavo was back in it. "You really do have the fastest feet on the planet!" said Brandon.

Early in the fourth quarter, Seth drove them to another touchdown. Paavo attempted to tie the score by going for the two-point conversion, but came up short.

"Rosemary still leads, 21-19 with about nine minutes to play," reported the announcer. "Still plenty of time!"

As the Paavo defense attempted to stop Rosemary, Seth stood next to Blair on the sideline.

"Son, you're playing a heck of a game tonight," said the coach. "But I don't think you've tossed one pass. I know you can throw the ball. I've seen you in practice. And we really need to mix it up a bit out there. Paavo's starting to figure us out."

Seth knew he had to tell Blair the truth. He lifted his hand. Blair looked at the swollen digit. Wisk noticed what was going on and peered over Blair's forearm.

"This happen during the game tonight?" asked Blair.

"Right before you put me in," said Seth, wincing as Blair examined the finger.

Blair sighed. "It sure looks broken."

Wisk stepped in for a closer look. "You've been playing the whole second half with it like that?"

"Yes sir," nodded Seth. He expected Wisk to yell at him, but the coach simply stood there as if trying to grasp quantum physics.

"Well," said Blair dejectedly, gazing out across the playing field, "we'd better get Danny ready to go back in."

"Coach," said Seth desperately, "I can still play."

"I don't want to see you seriously injure that hand," said Blair.

Seth struggled for words. "It's already broken!"

Wisk stepped up. *Here it comes. He's been waiting for the chance to get me out and Danny back in.*

"Bill, this kid has the fastest feet I've ever seen."

Seth could hardly believe his ears.

Blair thought for a long moment. "Have the trainer take a look at it."

The team trainer told Wisk that the finger looked broken, but it would require an x-ray to be sure. "There's a chance it's just sprained," said the trainer. "But I'd say it's a small chance."

He taped the middle finger to the finger next to it as a kind of splint.

"What did the trainer say?" asked Blair when they returned.

"He said it might only be sprained," blurted Wisk.

Blair was thoughtful again. Then he turned to Seth. "You've played a good game. You deserve a chance to finish it if you can."

The Paavo offense got the ball back on its own thirty with just over five minutes remaining. Seth inched them painfully down the field. As Coach Blair had predicted, Paavo had adjusted to Seth's style of play. They knew that the quarterback liked to run it himself on third down. They also knew he would not pass—or could not. As a result, Rosemary began to bring their linebackers and defensive backs up closer to the line, making it difficult for Paavo to gain much yardage on running plays. They began to wear down the Paavo offensive linemen, too.

"We've got to pass, just to get them to spread out the defense more," said Blair during a timeout. He called a pitch to Anderson, who would then pull up in the backfield and throw to one of the wide receivers heading down the sidelines. Unfortunately, a Rosemary linebacker broke through and sacked Anderson for a five-yard loss.

Still, Paavo inched along and they found themselves on the Rosemary twenty-three yard line—fourth down and fourteen to go—with a minute and a half left on the clock.

Wisk called time, consulted with Blair as the Paavo team drifted toward the sidelines. Then Wisk's voice blared out, "Hardy!"

Brandon looked as if he had been shot. Then he stood and jogged to the sideline. "Hardy, you're fresh. Here's what I want you to do. You're going in for Adams at left guard. Now, Kerrighan's your buddy, right?"

Brandon nodded.

"We've got to pick up at least fourteen yards. We're going to run the pitch to Anderson again, okay? Anderson's going to pass. Your job, Hardy, is to make sure no one gets through! You've got to protect your pal and Anderson! Can you do it?"

After a momentary pause, Brandon nodded enthusiastically.

"All right, then," said Wisk. "Let's go! And Hardy?"

Brandon turned, one foot on the field.

Wisk pointed to the bench. "Your helmet!"

With his helmet in place, Brandon took his spot in the line. Seth called out the signals, took the snap and pitched to Anderson. Anderson pulled up to pass, eying the ends who were sprinting down the sidelines. However, a Rosemary defender broke through around the left end and hit Anderson hard. The football popped out, bounced once on the ground and Seth lunged to snatch it. Defenders now poured in around the right end, too. Seth found himself caught in the middle. He could not race around either side, nor could he pass the ball downfield. As his eyes looked for an opening, he noticed one place where the line had not given way. Brandon powered forward, hunched over, his legs churning, pushing the defender to the left.

It was the only place to go.

Seth raced forward, leaped over his friend and into the Rosemary defensive backfield. The threat of a pass had spread out the defenders, and so he had room to sprint. His feet moved artfully, like lightning, the Irish music growing to a crescendo in his head.

"Touchdown, Paavo!" cried the announcer. And he sounded very enthusiastic.

Seth stood in the end zone, turned, and in that instant before being mobbed by his teammates, gazed to the place at the end of the bench where his father would have been standing. His father, who had loved football, who had loved his son, would have loved to have seen that touchdown, Seth thought. Of course, his father was not there.

But his mother was.

Eighteen

Music blared from strobe-lit speakers. Green and white balloons and crepe ribbons adorned the walls and ceiling of the gymnasium. Near the front hung a large poster:

Pilots 26, Mariners 21

"We're in the playoffs for sure," Brandon told Jenny, the girl with whom he had already shared several dances. "And by that time, Seth will probably have his splint off."

Seth held up his right hand, the middle finger immobilized by a thin, fiberboard strip, some blue foam wrap, and a few strips of white tape.

Danny would quarterback the team for the next few games. That was okay. They would make the post-season and perhaps get another shot at Drumlin. But it would be a long time before anyone forgot the Homecoming game.

"Maybe we should have all you guys start taking Irish dance lessons," Coach Blair had said during the post-game celebration. "We could do with a few more fast feet!"

And then Mrs. Kerrighan had driven her son to the emergency room.

"Mrs. Hardy called and asked if I wanted to sit with her in the parent section," Seth's mother had said as they rode toward the hospital. "I guess I thought that if I wasn't alone, maybe I could handle being at the game."

"How was it?" asked Seth. "Was it hard for you?"

"Not so bad," said Mrs. Kerrighan. "Mrs. Hardy is such a nice woman. And you were there." She paused. "And it felt like your dad was there, too, in a way."

Seth nodded. "What were you doing on the sidelines at the end?"

Mrs. Kerrighan smiled. "Brandon called his mother and told her you had a broken finger, so I had one of the security people escort me down there."

"Brandon had his cell phone with him on the sidelines?" Seth asked incredulously.

"Well, he didn't expect to get into the game!" Mrs. Kerrighan shrugged, and they both laughed.

As the music started again, a group of girls rushed up to Seth and pulled him out on the dance floor. He smiled. *Oh well.* They danced in a group, six girls and three boys, in a sea of celebrating teenagers.

"Let's see your moves, Seth!" called one of the girls.

Seth responded with a wave of his arms and a shake of his hips. The girl shook her head.

"Irish dance!"

Seth smiled and launched into his treble jig—to the beat of the blaring pop music.

A new girl appeared in their group and stood watching for a moment. "What's so special about that?" She launched into an imitation of what Seth had just done, getting about a quarter of it right, and throwing in some ballet, salsa and several moves that defied categorization.

Seth laughed. "Not bad for a beginner."

"That's because I'm a dancer," she said. "I pick things up quick!" He noticed then that it was Kimmy. She wore a simple yet attractive blue dress, unlike some of the gaudy outfits Seth had seen on many other girls at Homecoming. Her hair, straightened and pulled to the side, was adorned with a small, artificial flower. "Show me!"

He stood beside her, and in a few minutes, the two of them were doing the jig side-by-side as the Paavo student body clapped in time to the beat.

"Looks like Irish dance could get very popular around here in the near future," said Kimmy.

He smiled back at her. She *was* a good dancer. And as he watched her, he thought that this could get interesting.

Yes, this could get very interesting.

Dance of the Third-string Quarterback / 122

About the Author

Rod Vick has written for newspapers and magazines, has worked as an editor and has taught writing workshops and classes over the span of a quarter century. He is the author of *Kaylee's Choice*—which has become a favorite of Irish dancers of all ages—and the other books in the Kaylee O'Shay series. Mr. Vick was also the 2000 Wisconsin Teacher of the Year.

Rod Vick lives in Mukwonago, Wisconsin with his wife, Marsha, and children Haley and Joshua. An occasional speaker at conferences and orientation events, he also runs marathons, enthusiastically supports his children's dance and soccer passions, and pitches a pretty mean horseshoe.

Look for more books about Irish dance at www.kayleeoshay.com.

Enjoy these books by Rod Vick...

Kaylee's Choice
Ten-year-old Kaylee O'Shay's father wants her to be a soccer star like he was. But when Kaylee joins an Irish dance school, she is pulled in a different direction.

Green Storm
Kaylee O'Shay trains for her first feis, but decides she wants to play in one last soccer tournament, too. When her demanding dance teacher objects, Kaylee makes a decision that could jeopardize her dance career.

Fire & Metal
When twelve-year-old Kaylee O'Shay's parents announce the family is moving, she realizes that she will lose not only all of her best friends, but her beloved Irish dance school as well.

Christmas in Ireland
Kaylee O'Shay's Aunt Kat offers to fly the family to Ireland—but her secret motive for offering the trip will change all of their lives forever.

The Secret Ceili
Fourteen-year-old Kaylee is chosen to dance on a ceili team for the oireachtas. However, when Kaylee takes a job caring for horses on a nearby farm, her commitment to her teammates is threatened.

The Winds of Ireland
In a book that spans two years of Kaylee's tumultuous dance career, everything changes. Fate delivers a terrible blow, in the

form of a career-ending injury. However, Kaylee refuses to lose faith, defying her doctors while working with best friend Jackie to solve the mystery of the Lizzie Martin letter.

Isle of Green Fire
Seventeen-year-old Kaylee is a high school senior, and time is running out. Next fall, she will go off to college, and her Irish dance career will be over. She has one final chance to qualify for the World Championships in Ireland, but her injuries have kept her off the dance floor for months. As she struggles to regain her strength before her final Oireachtas, she finds herself closing in on Lizzie Martin's amazing secret.

Dance of Time
Dare McClaren and her friend Sammy are transported back in time to 1946 Chicago, where they try to save the life of a young dancer and look for clues to solve the riddle surrounding the disappearance of Dare's father.

The Dancer in the Painted Mask
A century in the future, the world of Irish dance is dominated by super clones who cannot think for themselves. At least that is what everyone has been led to believe. Then 15-year-old Wynn Jameson discovers a secret that will change the world—and make her a target.

The Irish Witch's Dress
An enchanted dance costume falls into the hands of 12-year-old Harp McCardle, who realizes she can use its magic as a shortcut to success. But Harp's learns her success comes with a price: the end of the world.

The Irish Witch's Tiara
Harp is now fourteen, and the Celtic witch has returned, looking for revenge. This time, Harp finds herself at a castle in Ireland where she must out-dance the sorceress or see the world plunged into a thousand-year ice age.

www.kayleeoshay.com

If you enjoyed *Dance of the Third-string Quarterback*, you might also like Rod Vick's *The Irish Witch's Dress* and its sequel, *The Irish Witch's Tiara*. The books feature chilling adventure, enduring friendships and a vengeful Celtic sorceress, all set against the colorful world of Irish dance. Here's a sneak peek of chapter one of *The Irish Witch's Dress*.

1

"We must keep our voices very low, lest they hear us," said John O'Malley to his eleven-year-old daughter. The two of them sat on the edge of her bed in the dark loft of the farm house. Had someone approached them from behind, the pair would have appeared to be staring at nothing at all, for their faces hovered inches from the painted wall boards. However, their eyes were actually fixed on a thin opening where a plank had shrunk, creating a viewing sliver that overlooked the kitchen and dining areas below.

"I don't see anything," whispered Katie.

"There's nothing to see—yet," said her father. "If they come, you'll know it. They usually arrive around midnight."

Katie knew the time must be close. She had gone to bed two hours ago, as had her mother, who slept in the large bedroom downstairs. Her father had come up and awakened her—as he had promised—just a few minutes ago. Katie still felt heavy with sleep, but excited, too. She had never seen *them* before, had always thought them the creation of adult storytellers bent on frightening or disciplining children.

A part of her wondered whether this was her father's mission as well. He had already told her they did not come every night, which provided a ready excuse if midnight arrived without the creatures. Yet, it was not like her father to spin yarns as a means of encouraging her cooperation.

But still…could something so fantastic be true? A shiver shook her. Although she wore a cotton nightgown that hung from her auburn curls to her toes, she now pulled the quilt from the bed around her shoulders as well.

"You're shaking," observed her father, speaking just loudly enough for her ears to hear. "Are you frightened?"

"Just cold," she whispered, although this was only partially true.

"You don't have anything to worry about, you know," he said. "The stone is ready. There won't be any mischief."

Although she could not see it in the dark, Katie had watched her father drizzle honey into a hole in the center of a flat stone that now sat on a bench in front of the hearth. A gift for the visitors. He had also left a bowl of milk.

Yet, as the minutes ticked by and she became more fully awake, Katie began to have second thoughts about their adventure. It frightened her to think that there might be a world of extraordinary beings that, under certain conditions, intersected with her own world. It occurred to Katie that if she crawled back into bed right now and succeeded in falling asleep, she could continue to pretend the creatures did not exist. Once she saw them, however, she would always have the knowledge that, on some nights, they were right there in her house while she and her parents slept.

Another shudder.

Katie was about to say *Maybe they're not coming* and had begun to inch her way back onto the center of the mattress, when she detected a slight movement in the darkness of the kitchen, something so subtle that she would have easily missed it had her eyes not been straining into the moonlight-tinged darkness for the past quarter-hour. Then she detected another movement and a soft sliding sound as a window opened. A dozen small bodies scrambled almost noiselessly across the sill, one bearing a glass lamp within which burned a candle. This bathed the room in a subtle, golden glow and offered a better look at the visitors. Katie bit down on a corner of the quilt to prevent herself from accidentally crying out.

The visitors had two arms and two legs, like humans, but were roughly one-third the size of a man, with skin the color of the full moon. Their eyes were large and dark with almost no whites showing, their fingers slender and nimble. They moved with the swiftness and grace of children, though their limbs were sinewy like working men, and their faces appeared ancient and vaguely sad. Katie noticed that all were bald and also bereft of facial hair. Their neat clothing appeared to have been deftly woven from the grasses, ferns and leaves of the surrounding countryside. The mob rushed to the milk bowl and honey stone, lapping from them like starving animals.

Katie moved her lips against her father's ear. "What are they?"

Her father turned his nose into her hair and spoke, almost inaudibly. "Fairies."

Katie's eyes widened. "I thought fairies had wings and were beautiful."

Mr. O'Malley smiled. "Legends say there are many different kinds of fairies. During the day, these fairies live in the streams and meadows. It's only at night that they come into people's houses."

She watched as the fairies finished with the bowl and the stone. Then one of them spoke in a low tone, difficult to hear, yet Katie felt certain it was an unfamiliar tongue. In response, half a dozen began to sweep the floor, pull down cobwebs, scrub the coffee pot, shovel ash from the fireplace. One even sat at Mr. O'Malley's desk, donned a pair of small, wire spectacles, and began paging through Mr. O'Malley's farm records, adding figures here, jotting notes there. The rest of the fairies scrambled out the window. Katie looked to her father in question.

"They're off to milk the cows, collect the eggs, make repairs. They're workers, all of them. They do it in exchange for the milk and honey."

Katie nodded but then asked, "What if you forget to put out the milk and honey?"

"Oh, then they get upset! They pull pranks. Maybe break a china cup. Hide a favorite book. Put a dead mouse in your shoe so that you find it when you go to slip it on in the morning."

Katie cringed.

"Why do they do it?" she asked. "All the work, I mean."

Her father watched them for a moment before speaking. "I think this race of fairies may owe some sort of debt to men. Probably the result of an ancient war. And I suspect they're not entirely happy about having to pay it. I'll wager that's why they misbehave whenever they are given an excuse."

Katie said nothing. Merely watching the small creatures efficiently clean the house was fascinating.

"But there's something else," her father continued. "I believe the fairies have helped *us* a bit more than they do most people. You see, one night this past spring, howling dogs woke me. Then I heard growling and some commotion out behind the sheds. Grabbed my gun, and when I came around the corner of the byre, there was one of the beasts, baring his teeth at me and struggling with something. Thought he had a chicken, so I shot him. When I came over to take a closer look, I saw it wasn't a chicken at all, but rather one of our little fairies lying on the ground, covered in teeth marks."

Katie let out a sympathetic sigh, and her father had to shush her. She knew packs of wild dogs were rare, but, according to her father, could be dangerous even to humans.

"First time I'd ever seen a fairy, and I had to slap myself in the cheeks a time or two to make sure I wasn't dreaming. I discovered that the little soul was alive, but barely. And unconscious. I carried him back to our house, placed him on a folded up blanket near the fireplace, cleaned his wounds as well as I could. While most of his injuries were bites, there was one rip in his leafy tunic that revealed a very narrow bruise. The leg beneath it appeared to be broken. Not a typical bite injury. I went to the sink to put water in the kettle for some tea for the little fellow, and that was where I noticed a scrap of leafy fabric caught on a nail sticking up from the windowsill. It matched the fabric of the fairy's smock. The unfortunate creature had caught himself on that nail while exiting, and the window had fallen onto his leg, breaking it. That was why he had been caught by the dogs. Usually the fairies are far too quick to be caught. His shattered leg had slowed him down. Naturally I felt awful. If I had fixed that nail earlier, the dog never would have caught him. But that was neither here nor there. I finished bandaging him up, splinted his leg, set some tea and warm broth near him, and tried to get a bit of sleep. When I woke at dawn, he was gone. I fixed the nail, of course. Since then, the fairies seem to have treated us exceptionally well. I suppose they figure I saved the little fellow's life. Or tried to."

He paused here and squinted through the space between the boards, wearing the subtle smile of a man who, despite evidence staring him in the face, still could not believe he had fairies frequently paying visits to his kitchen. Then he leaned back toward his daughter.

"I wanted you to see them because I figured it's time you know. They help keep the farm running, Katie. If anything ever happens to me, you must remember to put out the milk and honey."

"Nothing's going to happen to you," hissed Katie. "So you'll have to keep remembering yourself!"

"Oh, I don't intend to forget," her father continued. "Since your mother got sick, she hasn't been able to help out as much, you know. And her medicines are pretty expensive, so I had to let go the three fellows who had worked here since your grandfather passed, God rest his soul. There's a lot of land and cattle. Without the fairies to help tend to it all, I'd probably have to sell."

This raised another question. "Is the medicine helping?"

Mr. O'Malley smiled kindly. "Do you know what really helps your mother? It's when you dance for her! Oh, how her eyes light up! You're so good and light on your feet and it's almost like she forgets the pain for just a—"

At this point Mr. O'Malley stopped talking, for he realized that, in his enthusiasm, his voice had risen above the level of a whisper. The two squinted through the crack in the wall, but the kitchen was now dark again and as silent as the heart of a stone.

"Will they come back?" asked Katie. "I mean, now that they know we've seen them?"

Mr. O'Malley squeezed her tiny shoulders and tucked her under her blankets.

"I don't know, sweetheart. I don't know."

www.kayleeoshay.com

www.ingramcontent.com/pod-product-compliance
Lightning Source LLC
Chambersburg PA
CBHW031447040426
42444CB00007B/1006